GATHERING THE NeXt GENERATION

Essays on the Formation and Ministry of GenX Priests

Edited by N. J. A. Humphrey
Foreword by The Most Reverend Frank T. Griswold

MOREHOUSE PUBLISHING
HARRISBURG, PENNSYLVANIA

Morehouse Publishing
P.O. Box 1321
Harrisburg, PA 17105

Morehouse Publishing is a division of The Morehouse Group.

Printed in the United States of America

Cover design by Corey Kent

Library of Congress Cataloging-in-Publication Data

Gathering the next generation: essays on the formation and ministry of genX priests / edited by N.J.A. Humphrey ; foreword by Frank T. Griswold
    p.   cm
  Includes bibliographical references
  ISBN 0-8192-1832-4 (pbk. : alk. paper)
  1. Episcopal Church--Clergy--Appointment, call, and election.
2. Episcopal Church--Clergy--Office. 3. Generation X. I. Humphrey, N. J. A.

BX5965 .G3 2000
262'.14373--dc21
                                                                99-087590
                                                                CIP

Advance praise for *Gathering the NeXt Generation*

"The Episcopal Church goes into the new millennium in the hands of exciting, capable Christians, if this sample of the thinking of its younger clergy is to be believed! These essays represent different voices, but they are strong voices committed to building not just churches, but faith for the future."
—*Loren Mead, President Emeritus, The Alban Institute*

"The Gathering the NeXt Generation Initiative is one of the bright spots in the Episcopal Church. These essays are alive with passion, cultural sensitivity, thoughtfulness, and insight that is Christ-centered and sound. As someone who has been involved in the Episcopal Church for over thirty years, I found these words exhilarating and hopeful—and contagious. May this book go from 'strength to strength.'"
—*Carol Anderson, Rector, All Saints' Episcopal Church, Beverly Hills, California*

GATHERING THE NEXT GENERATION

Nathan JA Humphrey

Jennifer Baskerville-Burrows

Kate Moorehead

Earl —
Thank you for all
your support and
leadership.
Blessings,
Jamie E. L'Enfant†

CONTENTS

FOREWORD: FORWARD!

The Most Reverend Frank T. Griswold

W hen four Episcopal clergy under thirty-five realized that there were only some three hundred Episcopal priests in their age group, they formed an *ad hoc* committee and decided to do something about it. They said, "Let's see what needs to be done to make our church more hospitable to younger people who might consider vocations to ordained ministry." Their response is a contrast to people of my generation who often might fuss and say, "Well, why don't *they* fix it, or why don't *they* do something about it?" pointing a finger at the diocesan establishment or the bishop. In this case, this group of young clergy said, "Here's a problem; we have the freedom to do something about it ourselves." That spirit of independence—that capacity to act out of their own energy—is a very important gift to us as we look to the future.

Their discussions led to action and a conference—called "Gathering the NeXt Generation"—in June 1998 at Virginia Theological Seminary. Out of that gathering, in which I had the pleasure of participating, have developed several projects, among them the Young Priests Initiative, which focuses on encouraging vocations at an earlier age.

Throughout the conference, I was struck by the way this group was able to speak and listen to one another. During a plenary session I sat at the front of the church and could look at their faces and see the reaction, one to another, as they were sharing feelings and perceptions. One young priest said that he still could not accept the ordination of women and was glad to be at the conference, but had come in fear and trembling about whether he would be welcomed and accepted. And as he spoke, I looked into the faces of those who were listening, particularly the faces of the young ordained women present, and no one's eyes rolled. No one looked shocked or turned to a neighbor and whispered. This group could receive his comments with equanimity.

Shortly thereafter another priest said that he was gay and that this group was important to him because he had felt lonely and isolated and he felt supported by being with these people. I knew a number of clergy in the group for whom this was problematic, but again, no eyes rolled and there were no whispers or frowning looks.

I realized that this group was capable of a graced pluralism that my generation finds somewhat difficult, possibly because we grew up in a church where we had answers to everything. Or so we thought. The younger clergy realize that this is not the case. They have been shaped in a different historical and cultural situation from the one that shaped most of us in ordained ministry.

I do not meant to imply that they are without foundation or clear values, but that they recognize that their perceptions cannot be considered absolute, and that they must make room for "otherness" in ways that can be unsettling. And yet, what I saw in Virginia was the capability to look for Christ always in one another. They were not merely accepting that someone else had a different point of view but wanted to know the person behind the view and to recognize the Christ in him or her.

It is heartening that our younger generation's clergy speak a language of faith naturally and confidently. They are persons who pray deeply, whose intimacy with Christ is at the heart of their lives. And that depth of prayer, that intimacy with Christ is, I think, what gives them the freedom to be open and available to one another—even those who may hold points of view that differ markedly from their own. I hope that, in time, this spirit increasingly can become the spirit that binds us together as members of the Episcopal Church. In time, these young priests will be the leaders of the church, so doubtless it will happen.

This collection of essays by and about Generation X clergy gives a taste of their diversity of character and strength of faith. In these pages we see the rich resources we have in our younger clergy and a promising indication of what lies ahead for us as the Episcopal Church.

PREFACE

Conversation and Conversion

N. J. A. Humphrey

A s the editor of this project, I've had the pleasure of reading these essays, in their various forms, several times. Each time I have been impressed by the spirit, the love, and the passion these authors demonstrate for the gospel and for our brothers and sisters in Christ. Each essayist is committed to the church's mission "to restore . . . unity with God and each other in Christ" (*Book of Common Prayer* 855; henceforth, *BCP*). They have inspired and challenged me, and I am sure they will do the same for you.

I believe we have produced a book that will cut across many divides in the Episcopal Church: women and men, young and old, lay and ordained, liberal and conservative, gay and straight, Anglo-Catholic and evangelical, and everywhere in between. I hope you will take from this collection a greater appreciation of the riches of our church and the gifts each brings, in whatever state we were called (1 Cor. 7:17). From these places of calling, I hope we can begin a mutually converting conversation on mission and ministry in the next millennium. We can do this best, I believe, by following Jesus' example of sharing meals, challenging disciples and detractors alike, and simply being open to "all sorts and conditions" of humanity. Jesus' conversations with people, like the ones he had with Nicodemus or the woman at the well, had a profound impact on their lives (John 3–4). His conversation was converting. But it was also controversial.

One of the scandals of Christ's life was that he sat at table with pretty much anyone. The Pharisees complained that he "ate with sinners," but he also ate with Pharisees. I think of one dinnertime conversation in St. Luke's Gospel:

> One of the Pharisees asked him to eat with him, and he went into the Pharisee's house, and sat at table. And behold, a woman of the city, who was a sinner, when she learned that he was at table in the Pharisee's house, brought an alabaster flask of ointment; and standing behind him at his feet, weeping, she began to wet his feet with her tears, and wiped them with the hair of her head, and kissed his

feet, and anointed them with the ointment. Now when the Pharisee who had invited him saw it, he said to himself, "If this man were a prophet, he would have known who and what sort of woman this is who is touching him, for she is a sinner." And Jesus answering said to him, "Simon, I have something to say to you." And he answered, "What is it, Teacher?" "A certain creditor had two debtors; one owed five hundred denarii, and the other fifty. When they could not pay, he forgave them both. Now which of them will love him more?" Simon answered, "The one, I suppose, to whom he forgave more." And he said to him, "You have judged rightly." Then turning toward the woman he said to Simon, "Do you see this woman? I entered your house, you gave me no water for my feet, but she has wet my feet with her tears and wiped them with her hair. You gave me no kiss, but from the time I came in she has not ceased to kiss my feet. You did not anoint my head with oil, but she has anointed my feet with ointment. Therefore I tell you, her sins, which are many, are forgiven, for she loved much; but he who is forgiven little, loves little." And he said to her, "Your sins are forgiven." Then those who were at table with him began to say among themselves, "Who is this, who even forgives sins?" And he said to the woman, "Your faith has saved you; go in peace." (Luke 7:36-50, RSV)

Many of the people Jesus sat down with were changed when they got up. After their converting conversation with Jesus they may, in fact, have remained Pharisees or tax collectors or lepers, or, as in this passage, "sinners," but their lives were transformed by sharing a meal and a conversation with our Lord. The story does not tell us whether Simon also got up from that meal converted and forgiven, but I like to think that he did, because I identify with Simon.

Episcopalians share our Lord's Supper every Sunday, yet I think some of us have neglected to share in our Lord's Conversation. I hope it is not presumptuous to offer this book as a contribution to that conversation, but if it is, I am consoled by the thought that it is probably no more presumptuous than that alabaster jar.

The woman's jar contained fragrant ointment, and I hope our jar will be as fragrant. As to the contents of our jar, the first section, "Formation and Ordination," deals with issues surrounding the process for selecting and training the church's clergy as they relate to Generation X. This section begins, however, not with an essay by an Xer, but by someone born in England between the "silent" and "Boomer" generations of the United States.

One may wonder why we decided to include this person in the collection. His well-known name, of course, will appeal to a significant segment of the Episcopal Church's membership. But we invited Richard Kew to add his voice because we wanted to include an essay by someone with a passion for looking ahead, and who is concerned about helping form the next generation of lay and ordained leaders in this church. It helps that he agrees with our own general outlook, of course, but I hope his inclusion also indicates our desire to be in conversation not only with other Xers, but with those of every generation in the Episcopal Church. So we welcome Richard Kew's presence among us, and we are grateful to him for his participation in and enthusiasm for this project. The other two essays in this first section, both by Xers, address the discernment process from the perspective of a Commission on Ministry member and an aspirant.

The second section, "Formation and Ministry," addresses three issues in the shaping of young priestly vocations: a renewed emphasis on the curacy as a mentoring model, the importance of campus ministries in shaping and empowering young people, and an insider's view of bivocational ministry. Together, these essays give us a broader view of young people headed toward and beginning their ministries; they also highlight three areas of the church's ministry currently underfunded and overlooked by those whose sole model for a priest is the rector of a parish.

The third section, "The Changing Faces of Ordained Ministry," looks at four groups whose presence in the ordained ministry has grown significantly in this generation: Xers, African Americans, GLBT/Queer persons, and women. Each group has struggled for recognition and legitimacy, and each essay is written by a member of these groups. While some wish for theological reasons to exclude some members of these groups from access to the ordained ministries, as editor I have taken a pragmatic approach that I have found common among members of my generation, both liberal and conservative. Regardless of one's convictions on any particular issue, the fact is that significant numbers of people identify themselves with one or more of these groups, and it would be an incomplete picture of the Episcopal Church and its clergy if we cropped them out of the photo.

Finally, the fourth section, "Mission and Ministry for the New Millennium," addresses issues directly related to parish ministry by members of Generation X. The first essay is a realistic look at parish life, which challenges Xer priests to examine the intersection of their "personal" and "professional" lives. The final essay is an exciting account of a vibrant parish whose rector is an Xer, and it presents a creative vision of what parish ministry in the next millennium might look like.

It is my prayer that you will enjoy reading this collection of essays as much as I have enjoyed editing it. I also pray that you will not be bashful in sharing your reflections on these essays with one another and with us. To facilitate this conversation, I invite you to visit Gathering the NeXt Generation at www.gtng.org. You may also E-mail us as a group at GTNGBook@gtng.org, or separately through the E-mail addresses listed in the "Notes on Contributors."

Nathan James Augustine Humphrey
Feast of St. Augustine of Hippo, 1999

INTRODUCTION

Gathering the NeXt Generation

Christopher Martin

I n 1997 only 296 Episcopal clergy were under thirty-five—part of a group popularly known as "Generation X." That number was less than 3.5 percent of the more than eight thousand ordained people in full-time parish ministry. Inspired by this shocking statistic, in June 1998 a small group of GenX priests and seminarians put together a conference at Virginia Theological Seminary called "Gathering the NeXt Generation." As a result of the conference and the various initiatives that have come out of it, we are slowly discovering a common voice that is Christ-centered, Anglican, and uniquely GenX.

Nearly half of all Episcopal priests born in 1963 or after came to the conference. Above all, the reason so many attended was to meet their hunger for companionship. Many of these GenX priests expressed how refreshing it was simply to be around other priests their own age. For me, one of the most poignant moments of the conference came when, in a question-and-answer session with the presiding bishop, one of the participants, Chris Rankin-Williams, confessed his anxiety about coming to the conference. "I haven't been with people my own age since college," he said. "Right out of college I worked at a church where there was no one my age. Then, I was one of the youngest at my seminary and now I'm a priest at a church where, once again, there's no one my age. I was afraid I'd forget how to act."

He was not the only one with that fear. Most of us serve in dioceses where we are lucky if there are more than two or three priests in our age group. Furthermore, most of us serve in churches where there are few parishioners our own age. Although Xers make up nearly 30 percent of the population of the United States we comprise only about 20 percent of the Episcopal Church. To put it more personally, not one of the bridesmaids or groomsmen from my wedding participated in church or synagogue and very few of my social set from college did either. The Episcopal Church, along with all the mainline denominations, has done a poor job attracting and retaining Xers.

Conference attendees expressed universal pleasure in the unique experience of being with a group of people who were Xers *and* Christian *and* Episcopalian *and* priests. Before the conference, one person called me to sign up and said, "Frankly, the reason I'm coming to this is to see my friends." Many people came out of a desire either to establish or strengthen relationships with others like them. This hunger for collegiality and companionship was a definite characteristic of the conference and is characteristic of this entire generation of priests. But the conference also revealed much else about who we are, both as particular persons and as a generation. Above all, the experiences of planning the conference and of being together for that brief time demonstrated great entrepreneurial spirit and a desire to make our relationships in Christ stronger than the issues that might divide us. In this essay I reflect on these experiences and make some educated guesses about the major tasks we face together and the ways we might meet them.

The seed of the conference was planted when I read an article by Roland Jones in the November 10, 1996, issue of *The Living Church*, "A Shortage of Clergy Is Coming." The conventional wisdom of the church has been that we have too many clergy. While I was in seminary a good number of dioceses had shut down their ordination processes, because within those dioceses there were significantly more priests than churches that could hire them. Jones argued that such policies were shortsighted. Using data from the Church Pension Fund, he showed that there were a lot of active priests but that a disproportionate number were set to retire in the near future. To demonstrate the point a bar chart showed the number of active priests in each age category. What caught my eye was that fewer than five hundred priests were in the 26–35 age group.

I was fortunate enough to go to seminary with a good number of people in their twenties, although we were clearly in the minority. Even though we came from a wide variety of perspectives—geographical, socioeconomic, and theological—we enjoyed spending time together. A group of us routinely went out for conversation and beer after the weekly community Eucharist at Berkeley/Yale. One of the common themes in these discussions was a curiosity about other people our age pursuing ordination. After I read the Jones article I shared it with other young people who had often participated in those discussions. These included Christine McSpadden, Mike Kinman, and Bill Danaher.

After some discussion, the four of us decided to share this information with all of our peers, along with a proposal for a gathering. In the spring of 1997 we sent a letter, along with a brief questionnaire, to all priests under thirty-five. Half of those who received the questionnaires returned them, and half of this group volunteered to help create a conference or meeting. In the long run their volunteer efforts took many forms. At the conference, our peers presented fifteen small workshops as well as two papers to the plenary session. (Versions of these papers, by Scott Barker and Rock Schuler, appear in this essay collection.) In addition, many contributed by soliciting funds, by writing articles for diocesan newspapers, by aiding with logistics, and even by preparing a guide on fun things to do in the vicinity of Virginia Seminary. We also invited two guests. At the first morning session the Very Reverend Paul Zahl, dean of the Cathedral Church of the Advent in Birmingham, Alabama, presented a paper on Anglicanism. The Most Reverend Frank T. Griswold, who was there mostly to socialize and listen, also attended. With the exception of these two guests, the entire conference was filled with the work of our peers who volunteered their time and energy.

The participation of those at the conference demonstrated a deep desire to grow together in our relationships in Christ. The priests who attended came from all over, both geographically and theologically. People came from more than thirty states and all church provinces, including a contingent from Province IX (the Caribbean and Latin America). The participants were graduates of all eleven seminaries of the Episcopal Church; several had also attended other theological institutions such as Duke and Vanderbilt. Because I received the registrations in the months before the conference, I came to know many people ahead of time through phone conversations. One of the highlights of the conference for me was introducing a man who does not support the ordination of women (from the Diocese of Fort Worth, perhaps the most conservative in the country) to a woman who is active in gay and lesbian ministries (from the Diocese of Newark, perhaps the most liberal). The full range of opinion and conviction in the church was represented.

In the development and design of the conference we wanted to make sure that all voices and perspectives within the church were welcome. Furthermore, we wanted to be clear that people with different voices could speak and not be attacked for holding their views. In other words, we wanted to create an atmosphere of respectful creative tension. Our fear, and the fear of many coming to the conference, was that this creative tension would break into the sort of disagreements that right now devour so much of the church's energy and time. Yet we knew it would be inappropriate and heavy-handed to establish ground rules for conversation before we had even met one another. The success of the conference therefore depended on the quality and attitude of those who chose to attend, most of whom would be unknown to one another. In my opening remarks I said that coming to the conference made me feel like a partner in an arranged marriage. I knew I would need to be in a lifelong relationship with the other people at the conference and yet, having not met many of them in person, I didn't know whether I would get along with or even *like* them.

Throughout the conference there were differences and disagreements. One participant wondered aloud if the others really believed in Jesus. Another proclaimed the inevitable triumph of progressive liberal views. But even these more extreme views were, for the most part, heard and respected. The spirit of the gathering was best captured in an article co-written by three priests from Massachusetts, Beth Maynard, Margaret Schwarzer, and Bob Hooper, for their diocesan newspaper:

> Some will mistakenly think we are writing in evangelical code when we say that the gathering was Christ-centered, that the person of Jesus and his Gospel seemed to be the unselfconscious passion of speaker after speaker. We sensed among our peers a bracing, invigorating freshness—even urgency—about the power of and need for the basic Christian message. The Presiding Bishop, who was kind enough to accompany us on our journey, remarked on having noticed the same attitude. This was a group determined to keep the main thing the main thing.
>
> Others will mistakenly think we are telegraphing a liberal bent when we say that we honored the diversity within our ranks. But we did honor each other. We carefully listened to the experiences and truths of our brothers and sisters in Christ. . . . [W]e appreciated the fact that all of us were risking a considerable amount in the name of Christ. Each of us was moved when, more than once, we heard one person sincerely thanking another for the opportunity to see the church through his or her eyes. It happened over lunch, it happened in the many peer-led forums, it happened in small group sessions— it kept happening throughout the gathering.[1]

Many participants expressed similar observations in conversations after the conference and in the conference evaluations. After the conference, the presiding bishop was quoted as saying, "This group modeled for all of us how we ought to behave."[2]

"Gathering the NeXt Generation" showed new life in the church, and most of us who were there returned to our work optimistic and energized. But however successful the conference was, it was only a small start. After the meeting, Mike Kinman, one of the other organizers, said to me: "Now comes the hard part." Many of us who experienced the strong faith and high quality of the priests assembled in Virginia have since placed much of our hope for the future of the church in them. In one E-mail discussion with the other thirty or so leaders I wrote that we are like the servant who in the parable has been given five gold pieces. We can choose to bury the gold pieces in the sand or we can invest them to get five more.

Since the conference, the leaders have tried to include more people in this conversation and to discern prayerfully what we are called to do next. At the least, we know we are called to strengthen our relationships in Christ. In the time since the conference we have intentionally nurtured and expanded the network of relationships that resulted. In keeping with the entrepreneurial spirit of this group, more than thirty people have taken positions of leadership. Twenty are organizing regional gatherings based on the format of the 1998 conference. One of our peers has created a newsletter that keeps us in touch and that gives us a forum to discuss issues of common concern. Well over a hundred actively participate in online discussions. Plans are developing for another national gathering in 2001.

Several other initiatives have come out of the first gathering. The most obvious of these initiatives is this essay collection. Others include an initiative to recruit more young priests, a think tank, a conference on evangelism to young adults, and a mentoring network for seminarians. Most of these ideas are meant to expand our numbers and to continue the hard work of making our relationships in Christ more important than the issues that divide us. There is great value in this work. It can only help our ministry for us to feel the support and encouragement of our peers and to know that our numbers are growing. But I, for one, would not be satisfied to leave the work of this movement at that. Many of us do not want Gathering the NeXt Generation to become a club within the church or a mere support group. Rather, we hope it will be a network out of which will come significant efforts for the renewal of the church. Because this task is so new to us, and the future seems so uncertain, we are still determining together what those efforts might look like and what issues we are called to work on.

My best guess is that much of the work of this generation of priests will take place around two great themes, *mission* and *ecclesiology*. The mission of the church is "to restore all people to unity with God and each other in Christ" (*BCP* 855). Through these last few decades the church has not done as well as it could in pursuing that mission. By almost any measure, the Episcopal Church has experienced steady decline over the last thirty years. Despite the "Decade of Evangelism," the church has not been willing to change in any substantial way to reverse that decline. Rather, we seem to continue doing the things we have done in the past in the hopes that eventually the old ways of doing business will become effective again. They will not. The church needs to reaffirm its core mission: to bring people who do not know Christ into a genuine relationship with Christ.

The church needs to figure out how it can be genuinely evangelical, and I mean that in the original, not the political sense. Most people in the Episcopal Church still picture Jim and Tammy Faye Bakker if you mention the word *evangelism*. I'm convinced it will take hard, focused work by a wide range of people over an extended period for the church truly to accept that evangelism is at the heart of its call. Simply announcing bold goals of doubling "membership" or holding conferences on that theme will not suffice. A substantial part of the call of GenX priests may be to help bring about that transformation in mind-set so the church can more effectively proclaim Christ to a world desperately in need of the good news. This will require the work of Anglican Christians of all stripes, so that no life-giving manifestation of Anglican discipleship will be left out.

The experience of the conference leads me to think that the mission focus of GenX Episcopalians, in style and tone, will not be like anything we now know as evangelism. To borrow a phrase from Beth Maynard, one common experience of GenX priests is that we don't fit on the ideological map we've been given. The labels that may describe our elders often seem to miss much of our piety and personality. I believe the way we will go about mission will not fit the traditional maps either. If there is going to be a distinct characteristic of GenX mission, the conference indicates to me that it will be an emphasis on communion rather than doctrine or tradition. Those other elements will obviously be present, or there will be no genuine communion. But maintaining tradition for its own sake or using doctrine as a litmus test will not be closest to our hearts. What I believe is at our center is a desire, through Christ, to restore broken communion, not just with Anglicans and those in other denominations but, more important, with those in the world who do not yet walk in the way of the cross.

The other great theme, I believe, is ecclesiology. The conventional wisdom in the church, thanks in large part to the work of the Reverend Loren Mead, founder of the Alban Institute and author of *The Once and Future Church*, is that we are at the end of Christendom. Since Constantine, the theory goes, the Christian church has had a secure and well-defined role in Western society. That is no longer the case. We no longer live in a culture that can, without significant reservations, call itself Christian. One result of this shift is that the main field of mission has now become our own neighborhoods, and not foreign countries. Another result is that today's church is becoming increasingly like the pre-Constantinian church, living outside a culture that is either neutral or downright hostile.

If this is true—and it seems to me that, even if the analogies aren't perfect, we are facing a very different world—the norms of our common life must change if we are to survive and thrive. One of the most powerful moves in this direction is the reclaiming of baptismal ministry, a move clearly grounded in the liturgy of our 1979 *Book of Common Prayer*. (It is worth remembering we are the first generation to grow up with *this* book as *our Book of Common Prayer*.) The heart of this movement is the simple idea that all Christians are ministers by virtue of their baptism. The role of the ordained is not primarily to minister to the nonordained, but rather to support and encourage the baptized in their own ministry. This is a shift from the idea of the church as a community gathered around a minister to the church as a ministering community.

This sounds obvious and true on paper, and many churches claim this sort of ministry, but it is not the functional understanding of most parish churches. We are still heavily dependent on clergy to sustain much of what we call ministry. Many of us still seem to yearn for the old model of the English country parson in his parish church, the "Father" who will be there throughout our lives to help "hatch, match, and dispatch." That is the model of Christendom, but one that seems less appropriate for the world in which we find ourselves. Baptismal ministry is not just a nice idea. It needs to become central to our common understanding of what it means to be the church. Most of the church has the luxury of talking in these terms without changing behavior. For example, we invite an "expert" on baptismal ministry to speak at a diocesan convention, and we return to our parishes or diocesan offices with cutting-edge ideas in our heads but without cutting-edge actions. In the future we will not have that luxury. We must make this shift or most of our churches will cease to function.

If this shift does happen across the church—and there is no guarantee it will—then the role of the baptized will not be the only role under radical reconsideration. It is my hope that this shift to baptismal ministry will help us leave behind the hierarchical, bureaucratic model that may have served us well in midcentury but which now clearly hinders us. As Nathan Humphrey has written, in previously unpublished remarks:

The ministry of lay persons, bishops, priests, and deacons (following the order of the Catechism, *BCP* 855) is capable of a more theologically and biblically adequate understanding than the one that seems to inform the way we function now. This more adequate understanding is based not in the hierarchical power struggles of fallen humanity, but in a redeemed participation in the divine lovelife of the

Holy Trinity, inaugurated though not yet brought to completion in
the here-and-now. The Being-as-Communion of the Father, Son, and
Holy Spirit, after all, is not a "hierarchy" as some ancient heresies such
as Adoptionism explained it, but the co-equal, co-eternal, and con-
substantial interrelationship of three Persons who together are not a
plurality but a unity—and the source of all unity. By analogy, the laity
is to the threefold ordained ministry as the substance of God is to the
three Persons. In both cases, neither "is" without the other.

It seems to me that the church is now called to make this shift from a hierarchical to a trinitarian living-out of community. If this shift begins to
happen across the whole church, by God's grace, this generation of priests will
be among those starting to give real shape to a post-Christendom community of faith centered on the ministry of all the baptized.

Priests who are members of Generation X are certainly not alone in their
desire to transform the church, with God's help, so that it might pursue its
call more effectively. Most who are familiar with the conversations of the
church will hear in these essays echoes of Loren Mead, Andrew Weeks, Boone
Porter, John Zizioulas, Alexander Schmemann, and many others who for years
have been courageously bringing these issues to our attention. Our elders have
helped give us the language to speak about trends and issues many find trou-
bling. By giving us the words they have also given us hope and direction.

But such people are the exception and not the rule. Because the generations before ours have had such a clear vision of how to minister effectively
in their own time—I think particularly of the GI generation—and because
they have been so extraordinarily generous in their giving of time and money
to the church, we are able to continue, for now, to pretend as if things haven't
really changed that much. But by the time my generation assumes greater
leadership in the church, previous generations will have either passed on or
retired, and along with them, an entire era of Christian ministry.

The Right Reverend Paul Marshall, my liturgics professor in seminary,
liked to talk about the "Anglican Death Wish" so prominently displayed, for
example, when the church made little effort to accommodate the followers
of the Wesleys. When I first saw how few young priests were in the church it
seemed another instance of the "Anglican Death Wish." Congregational studies show that while a church may have a written mission statement, its mutually agreed contract is usually unwritten and unsaid. In many cases, the
unwritten mission of a church is "Let's grow old and die together." Is the
Episcopal Church as a whole starting to adopt that unwritten contract? Is the
fact that it has turned away or needlessly hassled so many of the young people

who have offered themselves for ordained ministry a reflection of its desire to "die with dignity," rather than to expend the effort to find new life in Christ?

The good news is that there are at least 136 people—the number of attendees at the conference—who refuse to accept that death contract and who are willing to work for the future growth and health of the Episcopal Church. And the number of people willing to take part in this task is growing, despite an environment that discourages it. In a time when the Episcopal Church often seems adrift and riven with internal conflict, this small group of young clergy may be a significant source of strength, renewal, and mission. As Christine McSpadden preached at a conference Eucharist, "we are called to be midwives, not euthanasiasts."

After the GTNG conference many of us returned to our ministry excited about the work we might do together. We are proud to talk to others about our experiences and our dreams and hopes for the church. Reactions to the conference and its work have been varied. Many are enthusiastic and supportive. For example, thirteen bishops, several rectors, and several church organizations helped fund the initial conference and have encouraged the subsequent initiatives. Some at the Episcopal Church Center and at the Church Pension Fund have gone out of their way to encourage our work. Others are very curious and track our work with interest. Morehouse was gracious enough to publish this book, and the newspapers and magazines of this church have done a good job covering the conference and its fruits.

Others, however, react to the conference with defensiveness. Underlying this reaction is suspicion of who we are and our motives for coming together. I and many of my peers, I believe, do not mind making our elders a little uncomfortable. Many of the church's assumptions need to be questioned. For us, the most obvious assumption is the predominant idea that people with prior "life experience" are the only ones who ought to be ordained—as if a person stops experiencing real life as soon as the bishop's hands are placed on the ordinand's head! Another is the shortsightedness in most dioceses that causes college chaplaincies to be the first item cut from the budget when money is tight. And there are others. Whenever one calls common assumptions into question some defensiveness is inevitable.

It is not our intention to complain about the state of the church and to do nothing. Neither is it our desire to form our own network and go about our business, heedless of the larger church. Rather, we want to work with the whole church to help prepare her to meet the challenges of the coming decades. We are only one generation, and we are a small one. In less than a decade the church will, I hope, begin ordaining people of a generation even more deeply informed by the pluralism and postmodernism of contemporary America, namely those now beginning to be called the "Millennials," who are still in elementary and high school. But for now, we are the generation of priests that in its bones knows most about this era now taking shape. What I would most like to hear from our elders is, "We have served the gospel faithfully for years and we have something still to teach you. You know and understand this new world in a way few of us do, and you have something to teach us. Let's work together by God's grace to help transform the Episcopal Church into a church prepared to thrive in the next millennium."

NOTES

1. "Perspectives: Gathering the Next Generation," *The Episcopal Times*, October 1998.
2. John Scheussler, "Executive Council Meets in Burlington, VT; Bishop Griswold: Young Clergy Models for Us All," *The Living Church*, July 5, 1998.

SECTION ONE

FORMATION AND ORDINATION

Tomorrow's World, Tomorrow's Church, Tomorrow's Leaders

Richard Kew

W atching too much of the *X-Files* over the years has probably contributed substantially to my sense of paranoia. But I sometimes wonder if there isn't a conspiracy around the Episcopal Church to make sure certain awkward questions are never asked. If there is, then clearly I am not in on the loop.

Somewhere around the mid-1980s, when I had passed my fortieth birthday and could no longer be considered young by any definition of that word, I began asking, "What are the criteria dioceses apply in selecting candidates for ordination?" This led naturally to, "Why are Episcopalians so determined to select for ordination almost everyone but the young, the energetic, and the entrepreneurial?" Interpreted as unworthy criticism of the ordination process, these questions were studiously ignored. Others who were asking the same questions received similar treatment.

More than a decade later we are able to see the devastating consequences of this myopia playing themselves out. What had been avoidable has in the meantime turned into a simmering, but still almost unacknowledged, crisis whose repercussions will be with us for many years. We have so ignored the younger end of our clergy force that today a mere 2 percent of our ordained leadership is under thirty-five. In an increasingly Generation X world, the Episcopal Church has burned almost all its generational bridges to the younger half of the population.

The last quarter-century may have brought greater breadth of gender and race into the church's ordained leadership, but it has been overwhelmingly at the expense of the young, the dynamic, and those with an evangelistic compulsion. What is required is imagination, creativity, and nothing short of an ecclesiastical equivalent of the Marshall Plan. If we do not begin this undertaking, then I suggest that the future looks bleak for the Episcopal Church. It ought to be the task of my generation, those of us in our late forties, fifties, and early sixties, not only to identify and mentor young leaders, but to let go of some of our leadership and make it possible for them to use their charisms in shaping tomorrow's church. If we do not, then we will have been guilty of thoughtless and shortsighted irresponsibility.

Blame for our plight can be liberally shared, but Commissions on Ministry must take their full share.[1] I believe commissions should be the diocesan visionaries. They should have been asking and seeking to answer the question, "What kind of clergy will tomorrow's missionary church need?" Instead, they have tended to become bureaucratic panels culling volunteers from the "Boomer" and "silent" generations, rather than seeking trailblazers from Generation X and the Millennial Generation. The system favors "company" men and women, which means that far too many type A personalities, the young, and entrepreneurs—people tomorrow's church most desperately needs—are politely turned away. A church mired in "process" does not want people who might upset the apple cart!

Shortsightedness prevails whichever way you slice it. For most dioceses "long-term" planning is more about meeting budget and divining which clergy slots will need to be filled in the next year or two, rather than developing an ongoing strategy to make themselves dynamic and missionary twenty-five years down the road. A by-product of such forethought would be a determined effort to find and train appropriate leadership. Instead, Commissions on Ministry persist in functioning like ecclesiastical civil-service examiners, driven by a well-oiled but cumbersome set of procedures that are unimaginatively applied.

We have now successfully built a rapidly aging clergy force, who despite its greater comprehensiveness is mostly equipped to maintain the church it received—and then to retire within a decade or two. Having spent more than twenty years traveling the length and breadth of North American Anglicanism, I sadly report that most of us presently in leadership cannot even conceive, let alone build, the sort of church that will speak and live with the power and grace of Christ in the emerging world.

Twice during the month I was writing this essay, I talked to diocesan staffs who had a burning vision to develop new congregations. These folks are utterly frustrated because they are unable to find the church-planters they need. During the same period I was informally approached by another diocese asking, because I have been at the front end of so many new ventures in the church, if I would be prepared to plant a new parish for them. I was flattered to be considered, but things have reached a sorry pass if in the absence of younger and more energetic clergy, a fiftysomething like me is courted to undertake this most exciting (and most exacting) of all missionary challenges.

In the last few paragraphs I have been spilling the bad news. I have merely diagnosed, not solved, a mammoth opportunity (packaged as a problem) that is before us. The solution would be relatively simple if all that was needed was to fill seminaries with enthusiastic and intelligent young men and women—but just being young and studying theology does not necessarily turn someone into the sort of priest that we really need. If tomorrow's church is to be healthy we should be diligently seeking, selecting, and training *transformational* leaders.

WHAT DO TRANSFORMATIONAL LEADERS LOOK LIKE?

Transformational leaders come in all shapes and sizes. They are people with a variety of gifts and skills, but what they have in common is that all they are and have has been surrendered to the service of Jesus Christ. A rich variety of characters and personalities, they are people doggedly determined obediently to go wherever God directs. Some will be church-planters, others skilled at bringing life to tired old parishes, and others still, the neatest pastors in the world.

A primary characteristic of such obedience is a willingness to lead regardless of criticism and personal cost. Anyone can gaze into the future, dream dreams, and see visions; what makes a leader is the ability to turn excellent ideas into working realities. This means being able to communicate the vision so others can share it—and help improve upon it. There are Lone Rangers aplenty, but those who can build a team around a God-given vision are worth their weight in gold. In Pauline terms this is "equipping the saints for the work of ministry" (Eph. 4:12). Leadership that transforms is leadership that builds a Christian community until it shines forth the love of Christ, is able to stand on its own feet, and has the capacity not just to maintain, but to multiply itself.

The most effective Christian leaders, whether they are in the limelight or live out their ministries in obscurity, are those who have learned to be *douloi*, slaves of Jesus Christ. Their audience is not the gallery but their Lord. What is important to *doulos* leaders is not the size of their salary package, or their career prospects, but a willingness to go where God sends them, to do what God requires of them—period.

One of the tragedies in the late-twentieth-century church has been a "professionalization" of the ministry that has raised up managers rather than leaders, therapists rather than pastors, maintainers rather than missioners. The modern church tends to be led by those who see ministry in terms of career rather than lifelong selfless abandonment to Jesus Christ. As we look around the church, it is not surprising then that transformation is the exception rather than the rule.

Christian leadership is deeply rooted in worship and personal devotion. Leaders who make a lasting difference have hearts formed and shaped in prayer.

Spirituality is not just something about which they talk—they live it, and it ener-
gizes their very being. Their personal integrity flows from a relationship with
God that is nurtured in prayer, contemplation, worship, and study—especially
of the scriptures. These are the characteristics of tomorrow's leaders, for these
qualifications are the ones that will ultimately make the difference.

I was not formed in a setting that took Catholic symbolism seriously;
therefore I came late to the notion that the priest's stole represents the yoke
of Christ. As the years have gone by, however, when I have put on my stole I
have found myself warming to this notion as both a gentle reminder and a
goad. It reminds me that I am called to carry a cross with the One who died
for me on the cross. It is a goad because it illustrates how far short I have
fallen, and how much I am in need of God's grace if I am to fulfill the fear-
ful responsibility that is at the core of the priesthood.[2]

In a world becoming far less friendly toward the Christian faith, tomorrow's Christian leaders are not entering a respected profession, but a vocation that requires them to "give and not to count the cost, to fight and not to
heed the wounds, to toil and not to seek for rest."[3] According to several people
charged with reviewing possible retirement patterns of clergy over the next
twenty to twenty-five years, if tomorrow's church is to affect culture in any
significant way we are going to need as many as five thousand young men and
women willing to lay aside ambition and affluence to take up the enormous
challenge of rebuilding.

One of the greatest challenges facing the church is how to identify, train,
form, deploy, and support such leaders. This task is going to mean a radical
rethinking of everything from diocesan ordination processes to our approach
to theological education. The more I ponder this enterprise, the more I conclude
that as the Christendom era becomes a memory, it will be increasingly to the
early church that we look for inspiration.[4] In those first centuries theology took
place not in academic captivity, but in the rough-and-tumble of pastoral and
missional life. This past reality provides significant clues to the correctives
needed if the present system is to meet the opportunities of a new millennium.

WHAT WILL TOMORROW'S WORLD AND CHURCH LOOK LIKE?

When asked several years ago by *The Christian Century* to comment on the
encounter between a fast-changing world and the churches, Loren Mead said:

> I don't see a lot of change. There's a theory about what happens when
> an institution hits the wall. The first stage is shock. The second is
> defensive reaction. The third is acknowledgement. Fourth is adapta-

tion. In my experience, the mainline churches . . . have hit a wall. A lot of things they thought would work aren't working. And as far as I can tell, some of the leaders have moved as far as defensive retreat. But an awful lot of people are in total denial and not even into shock yet. And I don't see many signs of acknowledging the depth of the problem or the crisis we're in the middle of.[5]

Things may not be quite as stuck as they were when Father Mead spoke these words, but the prevailing ecclesiastical mood still seems one of denial rather than embracing reality. While in some circles it might be slowly dawning that the world has become a very different place, few have grasped just how radical the changes are and how profound the implications will be for the Christian community. To use a sporting analogy, it is not only as if the rules were constantly being altered, but the shape and size of the field.

During the last third of the twentieth century we have been watching the demise of Christendom in the West. Its disappearance, like the mighty hull of the *Titanic* beneath the chill Atlantic, means we can no longer pretend that our culture is predominantly Judeo-Christian. Yet today's church, from national to parish levels, is still designed to pastor an environment shaped by Christendom, not to be a missionary people in a less than welcoming world. While wherever we look there are echoes and memories of our culture's Christian heritage, with each passing year the flavor of society becomes more pre-Constantinian.

In a few short years the Christian faith has become just one among many options in a pluralistic smorgasbord of offerings. During the next generation the huge task before the church is to work out how it might best reconfigure to address the gospel message to a society in which truth has been relativized, and respectability granted to a bewildering variety of secular and even pagan ideas. My generation of clergy, which straddles this transition out of Christendom, is not as equipped as Xers to work out the implications of this fact on the way the church fulfills its future ministry.

The world entered the twentieth century with the West riding high. Our Victorian forebears looked forward to a promising future in which Christianity had to prevail. This optimism was shattered as war, wealth, and competing ideologies did devastating damage. Empires have disappeared, and the faith has been rotting in what was once the Christian heartland. Meanwhile, fledgling churches planted as a result of the global and missionary vision of earlier generations have flourished beyond anyone's wildest dreams and are now the standard-bearers of the faith.

In the days ahead, high on our list of priorities must be discovering how to stabilize our position in the West, and how to turn ourselves back into a society-transforming force through Jesus Christ. This notion will make extraordinary spiritual and intellectual demands upon leaders and led alike. Equally daunting, however, is how we enable creative cooperation between Western churches and dynamic churches from the Global South[6] who want to share the challenges for gospel ministry appearing in our corner of God's vineyard.

If anything is to be learned from the Lambeth Conference of 1998, it is that our ministry dilemmas are to be shared, not kept to ourselves. But this sharing will require greater trust and humility than we seem able to muster at the moment. The creedal affirmation of belief in "one holy catholic and apostolic church" has, in the last few years, gone from being a nice ecclesial theory to a global reality that this coming generation must make work. Lambeth also illustrated how demanding it is for folks from an array of backgrounds and cultures to move forward in ministry together; perhaps Generation X's greater comfort with cultural variety is one of the gifts they bring to this process.

What makes this facet of tomorrow's challenge harder will be the difficulty of breaking yesterday's habits and old ways of thinking. Mission has become multidirectional, and no longer are resources—theological, material, and spiritual—going in the same direction. The older churches in the West desperately need a slice of spiritual dynamism from the younger churches, while the younger churches will continue to require resources of maturity and time. Learning to be respectful and to share will be more demanding than most imagine. Generation X may be in a better position to make this happen than those of us more set in older ways of thinking.

The approaching millennium has led pundits to paint numerous scenarios of the world's future. Whatever the differences in these scenarios, almost all agree that Western nations and their culture will never reign as supreme as they have. We are entering a period in which powers and civilizations will jostle for ascendancy, making tomorrow's world one of clashing ideals, ideas, values—and faiths.

A missionary church passionately determined to share its message is going to find itself rubbing up as never before against other faiths and religious philosophies. Christians have handled this experience in the past either by demonizing competing faiths, as at the time of the Crusades, or by caving in to modernity and surrendering distinctive Christian truths in the name of an insipid pluralism. Neither of these choices is honest dialogue. Honest and forthright dialogue will be of increasing importance if there is to be mutual understanding and respect rather than violent tension between people of differing faiths. We have seldom sought to relate to other religionists in this manner, which presents an enormous field of endeavor as we feel our way into a new future.

Another question before a new generation of leaders is whether the denomination as a way of organizing the Christian churches has a future. Products of the Reformation and Enlightenment, denominations that are focused around national offices and leadership seem, in many respects, to be leftovers from a bygone age. Series of experiments, formal and informal, with different approaches to connection and organization are increasingly taking place. While the loose-fitting and constantly overlapping networks facilitated by the communications revolution appear untidy and sometimes disorganized, they are far more adept at delivering a product than the classic structures of the past. Not only that, these new networks cut across traditional boundaries and barriers, and some seem to be in the process of creating promising new ecclesial amalgams.[7]

In the last twenty years denominations have gone from the sore-throat and runny-nose stage to grievous ill health. Instead of enabling mission, which is their intended function, they are being torn apart by everything from doctrinal and moral dissension to politics, style, and disagreement over fundamental articles of faith. Today, denominations are more of a drag than an aid to our efforts at bringing the gospel to a post-Christian culture. We have neither energy nor resources to divert from mission, in a spiritually hungry cultural and social environment, to prop up tired ecclesiastical structures. With each passing year denominations look more and more like dinosaurs in that last moment before they disappeared some sixty-five million years ago.

Christian congregations crave connectedness and will continue to combine in ways that provide fellowship and support to one another. As Anglicans we believe that the historic structures we have inherited are the finest way to enable connectedness, stability, and accountability. In the early years of the new millennium, one of the greatest challenges will be to discover how to disentangle ourselves from the corporate structures of the twentieth century, reconfiguring them to address an entirely new set of realities. This is something about which Generation X leaders need to be thinking seriously.

This task is likely to have an ecumenical dimension. If, as I think possible, we are in the process of seeing fragmentation of and peeling away from inherited denominational families, including the Episcopal Church, we can also expect a re-coalescing. We could find ourselves wrestling to enfold within our historic structure everyone from dissident Roman Catholics to independent community churches, while at the same time saying goodbye to some of our own congregations, or even seeing several distinct North American Anglican families come into being. I also suspect that the diocese, for a time at least, will cease to be a purely geographic entity as parishes link either on the basis of common heritage and interest, or through loyalty to a bishop from another part of the Anglican world.[8]

This consideration leads us to what I consider the most important question facing the church at the dawn of the third millennium: "What is our mission?" Our mission is to be faithful to God's mission. We are called to know Christ and to make Christ known. This simple slogan links the necessary integration of formation in Christ with proclamation of Christ. A few years ago a task force of the General Convention of which I was part expressed the nature of mission in the following way. While not perfect, it is a summary that a broad swath of Episcopalians could sign:

> God has lovingly and joyfully created heaven and earth. Human beings, however, have become alienated from the Triune God, turning away from God and one another. God, in love, seeks to heal the divisions that separate us from God and each other. In the incarnation, death, and resurrection of Jesus Christ, God provides the way by which all creation can be reunited with our loving and merciful Creator. In dying for us, Jesus Christ redeems us to new life. In him the Reign of God is made real and accessible for all. Empowered by the Holy Spirit, the Body of Christ present in the world today proclaims and lives out Jesus' work of reconciliation and redemption. The mission of the Church is thus to restore all people to unity with God and each other in Christ.[Catechism, *BCP* 855] As God sent Jesus into the world, we too are sent into the world.[9]

Having been sent, we are called to be missionary in a holistic manner, taking the transforming message of the risen Christ into all the world, beginning with the locality in which God has placed us. The front line of mission is always the local congregation, and this is the first place to invest our time, talent, and treasure. A concomitant of congregational health is growth. Healthy congregations have always spawned new congregations, undertaken works of mercy, raised up saints, brought comfort to the grieving and forgiveness to sinners, and served as centers of healing and as settings from which women and men have gone into all the world.

Tomorrow's healthy parishes will be no different—except that they will be doing these tasks in a world of almost constant transition. Our culture is crossing what Peter Drucker has called a sharp divide. Society is rearranging itself and its institutions. The kind of world being born is beyond the imagination of my parents and their contemporaries, all of whom were born in the early years of the twentieth century.[10] Their generation configured the church as we know it today; I hazard a guess that it will be my daughters' generation, Generation X, that will reconfigure the church for the next stage of its pilgrimage.

Let me end on a personal note. I was selected for ordination when I was twenty, ordained at the earliest possible age, and have had the privilege of using every phase of my adult life as an ordained servant of Jesus Christ. At times I have worried that my life experience has been so circumscribed. However, from my present perspective I can see how God was able to use the personal characteristics of each part of my life in the service of the kingdom.

Unbelievable as it seems from where I am sitting, the end of my ministry is now far closer than its beginning. If members of my generation are to be responsible stewards of these next few years, it is imperative that we do our best to identify, nurture, support, mentor, and set loose for service a new, young, and dynamic generation of leaders. As I look at the world today, in some respects I wish I were younger. The years ahead will not be easy. They will be fast-moving, exciting, sometimes excruciating, but overflowing with a totally different set of opportunities to know Christ—and to make Christ known.

NOTES

1. I write this as a member of the Commission on Ministry of the Diocese of Tennessee.

2. In his *Treatise on the Priesthood,* St. John Chrysostom writes that the priesthood "exceeds a kingdom as much as the spirit differs from the flesh" (3.1).

3. From the Prayer of St. Ignatius Loyola.

4. That this is already happening can be seen from the launch of the Ancient Christian Commentary on the Scriptures, a biblical commentary series that draws comment entirely from the church fathers. In the accompanying volume, *Reading Scripture with the Church Fathers* (Downers Grove, Ill.: InterVarsity Press, 1998), Christopher A. Hall of Eastern College draws a series of parallels between the apostolic and subapostolic ages and our own. "Extravagance and self-indulgence mark both ages, both without the church and within" (33).

5. "Learning Points: An Interview with Loren Mead," *The Christian Century,* March 23–30, 1994, quoted in Ronald E. Vallet and Charles E. Zech, *The Mainline Church's Funding Crisis* (Grand Rapids, Mich.: Eerdmans; Manlius, N.Y.: REV/Rose, 1995), 143.

6. The churches in what was once called the Third World now prefer to be known by a new regional name, the Global South. The Kuala Lumpur

Declaration, for instance, resulted from a meeting of the provinces of the Global South in 1997.

7. It is impossible to spell out the ecclesiological implications of such radical changes, should they happen. If you wish to monitor the debate and possibilities, then keep an eye on the Anglican Forum for the Future at www.episcopalian.org.

8. Along these lines, I think we may have reached a point of no return; this change in the diocese is going to happen for good or evil. I feel that after a decade or two of searching for alternatives, we are likely to move back toward remaking a diocese with different constituents, but with similar patterns to what we have now—but without a central bureaucracy.

9. This is part of the theological undergirding that emerged from the DO16 Task Force to Revision the Domestic and Foreign Missionary Society in the 1994–97 triennium. The group was asked to help rethink the world mission strategy of the Episcopal Church.

10. Peter Drucker spells out the implications of this trend in the first chapter of *Post-capitalist Society* (New York: HarperBusiness, 1993).

ORDINATION OR FORMATION

Which Comes First, the Chicken or the Egg?

Jamie E. L'Enfant

But the Lord said, "Do not plead that you are too young; for you are to go to whatever people I send you, and say whatever I tell you to say."
—Jeremiah 1:7 (REB)

We have all heard stories from older priests who describe their discernment process as "lunch with the bishop." If he liked you, you went to seminary. If he didn't, you went on to pursue some other profession. The face of the ordination process has certainly changed since then, as have the faces pursuing ordination. The process today is much more lengthy and elaborate, and aspirants for ordination are older and more diverse. While there is much to celebrate in the broader range of folks pursuing ordained ministry, there is still work to be done with our ordination process. Specifically, we need to recover an understanding of formation and vocation that allows for and facilitates the calling of young people to the priesthood.

This shift back toward young vocations is not simply a good idea; it is imperative for the life of the Episcopal Church. Consider the following alarming statistics from a July 1998 report by the Commission on Ministry Development of the Episcopal Church: Of the eight thousand clergy currently active in congregational ministry in the United States, only 296 are under the age of thirty-five. By 2015, more than 62 percent of the eight thousand currently active parochial clergy will be inactive. If this trend continues and the number of congregations needing clergy stays the same, there will be a shortfall in clergy of about 2,300 persons by 2015. Furthermore, Master of Divinity enrollments at the eleven accredited seminaries decreased 24 percent from 1968 to 1996. The Episcopal seminaries yield an average of only about 250 graduates per year, not all of whom proceed to ordination.

Not only do we need to be calling forth more clergy, but we especially need young clergy who can provide the years of service necessary to sustain the church through the vast number of clergy retirements and deaths expected in the near future. We find ourselves in a variation of the "Y2K bug" in that our shortsightedness in the last quarter of the twentieth century has led us to a crisis that demands immediate attention if we are to avert disaster in the next millennium.

Are our discernment processes flexible enough to adapt to these changing needs? My experience both going through the ordination process and serving on the Commission on Ministry for the last three years leads me to believe that our structures are inadequate and at times actually backward with respect to the issue of call. Instead of being proactive in recruiting and nurturing people for ordained vocations within the church, we sit back and adopt a defensive posture, waiting for people to come to us and present their argument as to why they believe God is calling them to be priests. We then try to discern "beyond a reasonable doubt," as it were, whether we agree that they are, in fact, called to the priesthood. The "evidence" for such a call usually consists of a polished, well-articulated eucharistic theology and a list of lay involvements in the parish. If the list of lay involvements extends too much into the community, then we suggest the aspirant pursue the diaconate instead of the priesthood.

The seemingly ideal aspirants fit the following profile. Having run the gamut of lay ministries, these aspirants have now come to the conclusion that they must pursue the priesthood in order to be faithful to God's call at this point in their lives. They speak well to their faith, and they have an admirable résumé of ministries and activities to undergird their statements of loyalty to the church. Developmentally, they have cleared many of life's hurdles. They are commended for their depth, maturity, and faith, and they are sent on to seminary.

While these second-vocation aspirants are certainly valuable to the life of the church, basing the ordination process solely on this model is severely limiting because it assumes that formation precedes ordination. The rector, the parish discernment committee, the bishop, the Commission on Ministry, and the Standing Committee are all watching for signs of spiritual maturity and vocational clarity, the litmus tests indicating that this person does indeed have a "calling" to the priesthood. But is this litmus-testing true discernment?

By definition this approach excludes young people, who have not yet had time to amass the quantity of lay ministries and "life experiences" needed to qualify for spiritual maturity or vocational clarity in the eyes of the interviewing committees. "You are so young; how could you possibly know you have a calling to the priesthood?" we ask younger people, as if an awareness of a calling were something one discovers only in the second half of life, like the Jungian process of living into one's shadow side.

What happened to all of those priests who just "lunched with the bishop"? Have they forgotten their own lack of experience and theological sophistication when they themselves went straight from college to seminary? Or is the very memory of their youth what keeps older clergy from supporting young vocations? Perhaps these clergy project their memories of themselves as young people onto young aspirants, thus frustrating young people's attempts to present themselves as viable aspirants. While recognizing that we are always in danger of projecting our own shadows onto others who share some of the very traits we dislike in ourselves, we must also be mindful of the prejudices we harbor against young people simply because of their age. Our twinges of embarrassment when thinking about our own early days do not justify a blanket dismissal of the young.

We must broaden our understanding of "spiritual maturity" and "vocational clarity" to allow for growth and development within and after the ordination process. We need only turn to the Bible to find a cast of characters shockingly lacking in spiritual maturity or vocational clarity who were, nevertheless, chosen by God for God's work. Moses was a murderer and tongue-tied sheep farmer, Jacob a scheming trickster, David a boy shepherd, Peter a self-protecting disciple who denied Jesus three times. The call process for the disciples consisted only of Jesus saying, "Follow me." And Jesus himself was an unlikely hero in the eyes of his contemporaries: a carpenter's (illegitimate) son from a backwater town in the Galilee. The Pharisees certainly objected to Jesus' apparent spiritual immaturity demonstrated in his lack of respect for the law, and his sense of vocation certainly gave them fits! How do we approach the task of discernment given this history from our sacred text?

Another challenge we face is that the current approach to the ordination process does not properly allow for the needs of the church. In addition to the desperate need for more young clergy, there is also a parallel need for more minority clergy, especially African American and Hispanic. We also need clergy of any ethnic origin who can speak Spanish. When the church takes the passive/defensive posture toward the process by waiting to see who comes forward to demonstrate his or her call, the church abdicates its own voice and fails in its responsibility.

Call must be mutual. The church must call forth people based on its own need, not only in a particular diocese, but for the church as a whole, perhaps extending beyond our national borders. And a person's interior sense of call cannot be the sole—or perhaps even the primary—criterion for determining whether he or she should move forward in the ordination process. The person seeking ordination must also articulate how his or her call fits the needs of the church. As Frederick Buechner states in his definition of *voca-*

tion in *Wishful Thinking: A Seeker's ABC:* "The place God calls you to is the place where your deep gladness and the world's deep hunger meet."[1] With a rapidly approaching clergy shortage and changing economic conditions in many parishes and missions, we are just beginning to come to terms with the needs of the church in the twenty-first century. Necessary developments such as nonparochial and bivocational clergy deployment—as well as continuing ecumenical possibilities—will continue to shape the needs of the church in the years ahead. We need clergy who are available, flexible, and creative.

The church has a responsibility to call forth people suited for this particular kind of ministry and a concurrent responsibility not to ordain others. Consider the number of people who demonstrate a calling to the priesthood but who have some limitation that precludes total availability to the church for priestly service—an inability to move from a certain geographical area, severe psychological issues, limited people skills, and so on. There are tragic cases of people being ordained and then having no place to serve. When the person's perceived validity of the call is used as the criterion for judgment at the expense of the needs of the church, we strike an imbalance that can lead to many problems. We need to reclaim the voice of the church and hold its needs before us as we practice discernment—without losing sight of the fact that the very nature of our task precludes us from simply developing a new kind of structure that replaces the current one. We cannot avoid the Spirit-led task of discernment that transcends our litmus tests, procedures, and quotas.

Part of reclaiming the voice of the church is returning to the notion of "raising up vocations." Interestingly, this idea has all but disappeared over the last thirty years or so. A retired priest ordained in the early 1960s told me recently that he always understood part of his charge as a priest to be to raise up other people for ordained ministry. During his thirty-six and a half years as a parish priest he sent five people to seminary to pursue the priesthood and one to pursue the diaconate. He understood those acts of sponsorship to be an integral part of his duty to the church.

I have been ordained for several years now, and I have never heard it suggested, either in my work on the Commission on Ministry or anywhere else, that part of my call is *encouraging* others to pursue ordination. On the contrary, we seem to work very hard to talk people out of any interest in ordination. For years the party line was "too many priests, not enough jobs." Even now that we recognize the fast-approaching clergy shortage, we still resist encouraging people, focusing instead on "the ministry of the laity" or "ministry in daily life."

While lifting up and supporting lay ministry is certainly worthwhile and necessary, we seem to be doing a disservice both to lay and ordained ministry with our current approach. While we have made progress by instituting more opportunities for laypeople to participate liturgically and parochially in the church, we still struggle with helping people make connections between what they hear on Sunday morning and what they do for the rest of the week. We discourage people from seeking ordained ministry, but we fail to help them realize that whatever they are currently doing is already ministry, be it a corporate career, a blue-collar job, or stay-at-home parenting. The ones who already know they are ministers are usually those already overextended with involvements in the church and in the world—the ones who run the risk of burnout. They are the 20 percent in the old "80/20 rule," the maxim that 20 percent of the people do 80 percent of the work. We need to protect them from burning out while reaching more people with the message that the servant leadership of Christ manifests itself in as many ways as there are people of faith.

But we have a long way to go, for we are struggling to keep existing clergy from burning out and losing faith in their own servant leadership. Have you noticed the message "I wouldn't wish this on anybody" creeping in overtly or covertly among clergy? A telling sign is that priests often dread the thought of their own children pursuing ordination. If the priesthood feels like a prison sentence, we need to reexamine the systems of our church.

I, too, am guilty of this attitude. I once found myself joking around with youth saying, "Oh, no, anything but that!" when someone mentioned an interest in the priesthood. The youth met me with blank stares and quizzical looks. I realized to my horror that they didn't understand the inside humor we clergy use in talking about our work as if it were some kind of punishment. They took my comment literally, and I realized that I had missed an important opportunity to affirm their interest and to encourage their consideration of such a vocation. I spoke irresponsibly and flippantly about a matter that could have a tremendous impact on the life of a young person, not to mention on the future life of the church. We have more influence over others than we realize.

Sadly, during this "Decade of Evangelism," encouraging young people to consider ordination has been neglected. When young people consider ordination, they are challenged to become more self-aware—become more aware of how God is working in their lives—and to take ownership of the journey of discernment. These challenges nurture a deeper faith commitment on the part of young people that will hopefully bear fruit in a sense of call to ministry, be it ordained or lay.

The current ordination process is easily more destructive of vocation and deeper faith commitment than constructive. Sponsoring presbyters are reluctant to encourage some aspirants (and usually *all* younger people) because they will get "eaten alive" by the Commission on Ministry or other discerning body. Some people who feel a strong sense of vocation to ordained ministry but who have had a profoundly negative experience with the ordination process have left the church completely. Hospitality is an easily neglected gift of the Spirit. "The Episcopal Church Welcomes You" needs to apply to all aspirants, whether they are accepted into the ordination process or redirected to lay ministry. Also, those of us who "survived" the ordination process are susceptible to inflicting our own wounds from the process onto the people we are called to serve. There is no room for hazing or "payback" intimidation in a process that is by definition intended to be Christ-centered and loving. These concerns are not a matter of structure, systems, or procedures, although they influence the overall healthiness of the process; rather, they are a matter of the Spirit that guides the discerning body.

My own story speaks to the influence guiding hands and well-placed words can have. In college I majored in philosophy, and as graduation approached I desperately endeavored to discern where to go next. I knew I wanted to go to graduate school, but I did not wish to pursue a doctorate in philosophy. I hoped to channel my interests into something more "practical," and "counseling" was the only term I could come up with. Clinical psychology and social work didn't seem quite right, and after talking with numerous professors, the director of religious studies suggested I look into divinity school. "What's that?" I asked, having only heard of people "going off to seminary." Soon thereafter I met with a recruiter from Duke Divinity School, and I decided to take a leap of faith and enroll as a graduate student seeking a Master of Theological Studies, a nonordination-track graduate degree.

At Duke I once again began talking with professors, one of whom strongly urged me to apply right away for CPE, Clinical Pastoral Education, to work as a chaplain at Duke Medical Center. I did so, and I was accepted for the following semester, a highly unusual occurrence for a first-year student not even seeking ordination.

My CPE supervisor was the first female priest I had ever met, and my life changed forever. During the course of my CPE unit, I began to see myself as a minister. Furthermore, I found myself opening up and blossoming at the idea of pursuing ordination, a seed planted by my supervisor with the knowing comment that "one day you are going to have to consider ordination." With her words I felt a sense of call very strongly, and I knew—as inchoate as the urging was—priesthood was to be my vocation.

This recurring theme in my vocational path—of other people recognizing where I was heading long before I did, and pointing me in the appropriate direction—speaks to the impact such initiative has. I never would have pursued divinity school or CPE had others whom I trusted not suggested them to me. I was twenty-three years old when I began the first steps in the ordination process, and it took some time before I was ready to pursue the process in a formal way. Although my rector was supportive, the parish discernment committee he convened for me thought I needed more time. I was angry at questions like, "Have you considered nursing?" but I came to accept that I was so new to my "faith voice"—I really had no ministerial identity prior to working as a hospital chaplain in CPE—that I really did need some time to develop my calling.

In retrospect, I was very grateful for this delay, not because I wasn't called, but because I was told by a friend on the Commission on Ministry that I "never would have made it" past the initial interview. (Again the phrase "eaten alive" comes to mind.) I might have been one of those ordination-process fatalities, driven out of the church by what felt like cruel exclusion. I would have been expected to articulate clearly and accurately a developed sense of call based on a eucharistically centered, parish-based model of the priesthood before beginning any formal formation. Could the process have been adjusted for someone in my situation?

The way things were then, the answer was no. Unfortunately, things don't appear to have changed much since then. Perhaps Commissions on Ministry are unwilling to be flexible because they want to be fair. They don't want to show anyone "preferential treatment" or to set potentially problematic precedents. Yet shouldn't every child of God receive "preferential treatment" in the sense of personalized attention? Isn't flexibility a part of hospitality as we endeavor to "seek and serve Christ in all persons" and "respect the dignity of every human being" (The Baptismal Covenant, BCP 305)? How do we balance the consistency of a process with the specificity of particular situations? The Spirit can be maddeningly inconsistent!

Meanwhile, during the next year and a half, I switched to the Master of Divinity degree program and did a field-education placement in a parish. This experience allowed me to grow and develop tremendously, so much so that when the parish discernment committee reconvened eighteen months later, they gave me an enthusiastic recommendation. I then entered the process formally, completing my M.Div. at Duke and a Master of Sacred Theology at the General Theological Seminary in New York. Although I was in the highly unusual position of having my seminary education and CPE precede the ordination process, I was supported and approved by the bishop, by the Commission on Ministry, and by the Standing Committee, and was ordained deacon and priest when canonically appropriate. So in my case, at least, there was a happy ending to my ordination-process story and a happy beginning to my life in ordained ministry. But others have not been so blessed.

When looking at the "letter of the law," my story is a notable exception to the current design of the ordination process in most dioceses. But when looking at the "spirit of the law," I had a very full and complete discernment process that allowed me to grow into an understanding of my call and to artic- ulate that call clearly—despite the structure of the process. Although when I began pursuing ordination, I was hardly able to articulate my faith, much less my calling to the priesthood, my education at Duke Divinity School and my parish field-education experience enabled me to catch up quickly. Further- more, because I grew into a sense of myself as an aspirant for the priesthood as I grew into a sense of myself as an individuated adult, the connection between my identity as a priest and my sense of self is inseparable. I have an impenetrable level of dedication to serving the church as a priest for the next thirty (plus) years because I can no more divorce myself from my identity as a priest than I can divorce myself from my own soul.

And my experience and attitude mirror that of my (very few) peers. At the "Gathering the NeXt Generation" conference, the earnestness of the par- ticipants and their level of dedication to the church humbled and inspired me. Anyone despairing over the future of the church would have felt new hope at the sight of the energy and spirit present at that conference.

Yet we don't trust the intimations from young people who feel called to pursue the priesthood. In my diocese, for instance, the ordination process is structured in such a way that the first real opportunity for growth, learning, and formation comes during an intern year, which takes place *after* the person has been approved by the rector, parish discernment committee, bishop, and Commission on Ministry. Although other dioceses have mini- internships prior to initial interviewing, there is little opportunity for actual growth and formation prior to formal interviewing. We expect aspirants for ordained ministry to be spiritually and developmentally mature at the outset. Once again we see that formation is presumed to precede the ordination process. People need to gain formation and development on their own and with mentors before beginning the steps to ordination. If young people had the opportunity to experience what I did—theology classes and field educa- tion—then they might have a chance to develop sufficiently to journey through the ordination process as it is currently structured.

But perhaps there are some changes we could make. College students are typically able to relocate in order to attend graduate school. Is it possible for college graduates to attend seminary in one diocese as part of a discernment process in another diocese? Or must we continue to put people through many hoops before sending them to seminary? Seminaries could use the increased enrollment, and it is an excellent environment for formation, as well as evaluation.

Some might object that the high cost of seminary dissuades people who cannot be guaranteed they will be ordained, and the diocesan process ensures that we don't waste people's resources on unnecessary professional education. But if people choose to go to seminary, knowing it is without any guarantee of ordination, their formation and education there will not be wasted, whether they become ordained or not. If we are really serious about equipping and empowering the laity for ministry, then why shouldn't we encourage more people to receive seminary training? And why shouldn't the accompanying stewardship issues concern us, as well?

A summer job as a paralegal helped me discern beyond a shadow of a doubt that I was not called to be a lawyer. Could those dioceses that have an internship year move it to an earlier stage in the process, so that young people could get more of a sense of the daily life of a parish priest? This experience could be enormously helpful for discernment.

But beyond mere structural adjustments, the ordination process needs to strengthen its connection to its mission of discernment in a spirit of hospitality. The church needs to embrace, nurture, and encourage talented young people who want to pursue a life of ordained ministry in the church. Instead, we neglect even to present the priesthood as a possibility. To those who manage to show interest anyway, we sometimes drive them to other denominations not quite so unreceptive—or worse yet, away from the church completely. If we could adapt the discernment process for ordination to make it more appropriate for young people in or just out of college, then we can make far better use of the talents entrusted to us. Instead of burying those talents in the sand, we could multiply their value, as the trustworthy servant did in the parable of the talents (Matt. 25:21).

We must be flexible enough to adjust our processes to the circumstances. We must be people guided by the spirit of the law, which takes creative energy. Happily, exciting changes are already starting to take place. Dioceses such as Atlanta are experimenting with separate discernment steps for people under the age of twenty-three. St. Michael and All Angels parish in Dallas is beginning a comprehensive, six-week summer intern program for college sophomores and juniors entitled "Pathways to Ministry," which carries an honorarium, housing, and living costs. And in December 1998, Presiding Bishop Frank Griswold, along with eight other clergy and a layperson, met with Bishops

Robert Duncan of Pittsburgh, Peter Lee of Virginia, and Thomas Shaw of Massachusetts to discuss ways of increasing the number of young priests in the Episcopal Church. Named "The Young Priests Initiative," this project ended with each bishop agreeing to form pilot programs tailored to the needs and gifts of their particular dioceses that encourage and expedite young vocations to ordained ministry.

As the Bible and our calendar of saints clearly show us, God repeatedly calls forth young—and otherwise unlikely—candidates for special kinds of ministry, as the verse from Jeremiah at the beginning of this essay illustrates. But we in the church have grown suspicious of anyone who is young or different in some way. Interestingly, we trust young people to grow into an understanding of what it means to be a doctor or lawyer or teacher or parent—and we trust them to acquire the necessary job skills—but we don't trust them to be similarly formed by the process of becoming a priest. Can we afford such hubris?

I was no more "called" when I was accepted into the process than when I first felt a sense of it—I could just articulate it more clearly. And while I certainly developed emotionally and spiritually as a person while working toward ordination, in retrospect I firmly believe that the process need not have feared my youth. We seem to have lost a sense of trust that young people are capable of making a commitment, capable of having a vocational calling that can "stick" at such a young age. We need to recover a sense of trust in God's hand at work. In the passage from Jeremiah, it is the speaker who does not trust his own self to be worthy of ministry. We seem to be sending the message that the church itself does not believe our own young people worthy of ordained ministry. We are in danger of hurting ourselves through our arrogance. The future of our church depends on the dedication of ordained servants who will help lead the church through the radical changes the new millennium promises to bring. Will we be ready?

Formation is a lifelong process, and ordination is one way of living out a life of faith. To expect one to precede the other is to misunderstand the nature of calling, which is, after all, an invitation. The calling to the priesthood is an invitation from God to live out a life of faith in service to the church through preaching the word and administering the sacraments. The calling to the priesthood is also an invitation from the church as represented by the bishop and other members of the discernment process. We need to reexamine our responsibility with that invitation, remembering the charge with which we have been entrusted, and to trust in God's grace and presence within all of the members of the body of Christ, especially the young ones.

> *Let no one look down on you because you are young, but set an example for the believers in speech, in life, in love, in faith, and in purity.*
> —1 Timothy 4:12

NOTES

1. Frederick Buechner, *Wishful Thinking: A Seeker's ABC* (New York: Harper-Collins, 1993), 119.

TRUSTING THE PROCESS

N. J. A. Humphrey

When I became an aspirant, the first thing I was told was "Trust the process." I tried. But when it came right down to it, I didn't trust the discernment process. Don't get me wrong; it's not that I *couldn't* trust the process, or that I *wouldn't* trust the process; it's just that I didn't trust the process. I went up and down on the teeter-totter of trust. Some days I trusted the process more than other days. Many days I sat in the dust at the bottom of that see-saw, wondering how I could trust a process that I didn't feel was on the other end. Slowly, I came to believe that there was an imbalance in the way I related to the process, and perhaps also the way the process related to me.

I feel, I then thought, like that guy in Matthew 7. I've got this big log called mistrust in my eye, but all I can do is look at this silly speck in the process's eye, and I see it quite clearly. I've focused my eye on it for so long that I can even tell whether it's a pine needle or an oak sliver. Yet every time I've tried to reach out my hand to help the process remove it, my arm keeps bumping against my log. For a long time, I tried to reach under or over that log, not even fully aware it was in my eye; I even thought the log was an obstacle the process had intentionally put in my way! Then, once I realized the log was in my eye, I thought, "Well, once I get the speck out of the process's eye, it'll take the log out of mine."

But that's not the solution Jesus proclaims. Jesus says, "First take the log out of your own eye, and then you will see clearly to take the speck out of your sibling's eye" (Matt. 7:5, NASB, adapted). And that's the intention of this essay, with one minor adjustment: once I've shown how God has begun to help me take the log out of my eye, I won't try to take the speck out of the process's eye; that's my sibling's job, and I no longer wish to feel responsible for that task. Thinking about that job has only made me anxious, and we all know a shaky finger isn't any good at removing specks from other peoples' eyes. Instead, I'll try to describe where I see that speck, so that the process may use its own finger, if it wants, to remove it.

DESCRIBING MY LOG: JESUS' CALL TO CONVERSION

Jesus' exhortation to remove the log from our own eyes is nothing less than a call to conversion. Although this call is directed toward people who, like me, are quick to evaluate, analyze, and judge others, on a deeper level it's about continual conversion to loving God with all our heart, soul, and mind, and our neighbor as ourselves (Luke 10:27 and parallels).

Each of us has different logs in our eyes, and I definitely have more than just the log of mistrust in mine. But that's the one that has kept me from loving God and neighbor more deeply in the discernment process. Once I became more deeply aware of my feelings, I recognized a call to conversion, not only in the way I relate to the process, but also in the way I relate to God and neighbor. Before I can articulate my vision of conversion, though, I must describe the log of mistrust through which I received that call to conversion.

No one can trust someone or something they fear. And I fear the process. I'm afraid of it, because I've felt, at times, that it has the power of life and death over me, the power to determine my fate. But when I worship God, especially when I'm on retreat at a monastery, away from sponsoring parish, internship parish, or lay committee reports, I see that God is the one with the power, not lording it over me "as the Gentiles do," but pouring out upon me the power of love (Luke 22:23–27). I know Jesus will never leave me or forsake me (Heb. 13:5). I realize, at least in my head, that whatever happens to me in the process, I'm not powerless. I just need to trust that God will work as powerfully in my neighbors' lives as God has in mine. But too often, when I look at the process, I feel as if I am lost in a stormy sea, and that I will sink.

In these moments, I am Peter on the Sea of Galilee (Matt. 14:22–33). Jesus has said, "Come!" I have stepped out on the water in faith. I'm exuberant. Exalted. It's the greatest feeling of liberation and fulfillment that I've ever felt. I'm stepping toward my Lord, whose love makes me who I am created to be and who empowers me to share that love with others. But then I look down. I see the whitecaps. I'm suddenly aware of the freezing wind lashing my face, and it's not the "Spirit of God moving over the surface of the waters," either (Gen. 1:2, NASB). And predictably, I begin to sink—not slowly, but fast. I only have enough time to scream out, "Lord, save me!" But even before the words are out of my mouth, Jesus is there, reaching out his hands, holding me tightly, bracing me against the wind. We're still out there, standing on the water. And I'm crying like a baby. I want to go back to the boat, where it's safe, but Jesus still whispers in my ear, "Come."

Unlike Peter, this experience hasn't happened to me just once. It's the story of my faith. Maybe God is trying to teach me something about the nature of trusting Jesus through learning to trust my brothers and sisters in Christ; maybe there's a lesson God would like me to teach my brothers and sisters in Christ about trusting in each other.

Either way, I often feel that God is making it tougher than it needs to be. I recently read *Tuesdays with Morrie,* a true story about a man with Lou Gehrig's disease and his conversations with a former student about life. At one point, Morrie is asked what he thinks of the Book of Job. " 'I think,' he says, smiling, 'God overdid it.' "[1] In my own case, however, maybe it's not God who's overdoing it; perhaps it's us, and by "us" I mean both the process and me. Maybe we're overdoing it, at least in part, by not trusting each other. So, why don't I trust the process? Perhaps if I understand why I don't, I can begin to understand how I can. So here goes.

How can I trust a process that doesn't trust me? It hurts to be told by people involved in my process that I don't have any life experience, that I haven't suffered. In my short twenty-five years on this earth, I've had a family member who's attempted suicide, lived with mental illness in my family, seen my parents go bankrupt from helping others, become the child of divorced parents, had a cancer scare . . . and I was picked on by my fourth-grade class, too! I shouldn't have to "prove" that I've suffered or that I've lived. Just being alive proves it all. Such questions imply that people only begin to feel pain (or learn from it) after thirty, and that this disqualifies younger people from valid or effective ministry. I find it ironic that these questions come from some of the same people who used to say, "Don't trust anyone over thirty." Perhaps these folks know better now, and it really is the under-thirties who can't be trusted. But wouldn't that be convenient? Are the people who ask these questions unaware of their critique or are they intentionally trying to provoke young people? If it's the latter, does this kind of provocation truly aid discernment?

How can I trust a process that doesn't respect me? It hurts to be condescended to, as if I was some pet project or wayward child. One influential person in my process told me, "If I had my say with you, I'd make you be a garbageman for a year or two." This person's point was that I needed more "real-life" experience. Point well taken. But should we be playing God with people's lives? I felt like saying, "I'll tell you what: you quit your high-paying, white-collar job and go to work with me for two years as a sanitation worker, and I'll do it." I wonder if those in charge of the process would be so quick to assume they knew what was best for me if they had to do it themselves.

How can I trust a process that doesn't value me? Strange as it may seem, it actually hurts when I'm asked, "Why are you in such a hurry? You're so young. Why don't you enjoy it? I wish I'd enjoyed my youth more." This question implies that I'm presumptuous for wanting to give myself to the service of others through a lifetime of ordained ministry. It's as if I'm being asked, "Why not spend some time being a slacker?" I find it ironic to hear these questions from the same people who complain about their twenty-something "slacker" kids graduating from college and immediately moving back into the house. I'm at that time in life now when I not only want to go faster, but it's an economic necessity to do so. For the first two years out of graduate school, for instance, I was getting paid $1,250 a month, $725 of which went to student loans and $450 to rent. That left $75 for the telephone bill, car, and medical insurance, and let's not forget food. How can I slow down, enjoy my youth more? I know a lot of people have it much worse. And I know many of my elders faced similar struggles when they were young; perhaps that's why they couldn't enjoy *their* youths more. I'll never be rich, and I don't want to be; if I did, I'd have gone to law school with my other classmates, as I'd originally planned. I decided to make these sacrifices because I believe the church is worth it. But when I'm expected to spend my life scraping by on a wing and a prayer while the process ages me like cheese, I wonder: Is this what the church believes *I'm* worth?

My hunch is that most of the people who ask questions like, "How can you be called—you're so young?" or "How can you relate to others when you haven't suffered much?" aren't aware how offensive and hurtful these questions are to Xers, how biased against young people they seem. Maybe I'm being oversensitive, but do people in charge of the process routinely ask, "How can you relate to white people when you're so black?" The people who ask these questions need to know that as an Xer, I perceive them as official representatives of the church's attitude toward young people. These questions make it seem as if we have to prove not just that we "deserve" ordination, but that we deserve to be in the church at all. But since when did ministry, lay or ordained, become a matter of desert? We might as well be told, "How dare you offer ministry!" Imagine if young people offering themselves for lay ministry were asked the same questions. We'd have very few Xers in the church at all. On second thought, perhaps we should ask ourselves if they *are* being asked these questions. We don't have many Xers in the church.

As these examples show, I'm angry with people who don't know what's going on in my life but assume they know all about me. There's precious little empathy in the process, especially for young people, and as a result I've had precious little empathy for the process.

I could brood, let my anger seep in deep, and hold a grudge. Others have. But I know I can't demand that the process empathize with me until I try to empathize with it. How can I expect the process to have a heart of flesh if I have a heart of stone (Ezek. 11:19 and 36:26)? That's why I want to begin getting this pesky log of mistrust out of my eye.

For when I look at how I *want* to feel, I don't want to be angry. I want to be able to love, trust, and respect my brothers and sisters in Christ. They've been given an extraordinarily important and extraordinarily difficult ministry. I hate that the process tacitly fosters adversarial relationships rather than cooperative ones. Even when there is conflict, what happened to that attitude of discernment so beautifully formulated in Acts 15:28: "For it seemed good to the Holy Spirit and to us . . ." (NASB)? Maybe it's as difficult for the process to trust me as it is for me to trust the process. I don't know. We don't talk much.

REMOVING MY LOG: A VISION OF CONVERSION

Jesus said that once we began to take the logs out of our own eyes, we would begin to see more clearly. As I work on removing this log of mistrust, I am getting a clearer vision of the areas of my life still in need of conversion. By grace, I am hearing Jesus' call to conversion, and God has led me to people who've assisted in pulling that log out and sending it to the sawmill, where it belongs. God has been faithful, and the more I have become aware of God's faithfulness, the more I have been able to trust that if God's grace is sufficient for me, it will be sufficient for the process as well—speck or no speck. God's grace has not stopped there, however. In addition to becoming more aware of the areas of my life still in need of conversion, I have also become more aware of the larger meaning of conversion, and that awareness has affected the way I see and understand the speck in the process's eye.

The purpose of my life is to love God and neighbor (Luke 10:27). And in my reading of the parable of the Good Samaritan, everyone is my neighbor (10:25–37). This includes the people charged with carrying out the ministry of the discernment process. In my experience, I have found that the key to loving God and neighbor has been learning to trust God and neighbor.

Trust is another word for faith. As mentioned earlier, throughout my discernment process I have often felt like Peter, sinking beneath the stormy Sea of Galilee. When Jesus stretches out his hand and says to Peter, "O you of little faith, why did you doubt?" I hear those words directed at me (Matt. 14:31, NASB). But as I hear them, I also see the face of Jesus, not angry and scolding, not disappointed or disapproving, but with a Mona Lisa smile and a faint chuckle in his throat. At those moments, I cry out with tears in the words of another man in the Gospel: "Lord, I believe; help thou mine unbelief" (Mark 9:24, KJV).

My friends have often described the discernment process as a sort of "sink or swim" experience. But more truthfully, it's a sink or trust experience. These "Petrine moments," as I call them, are for me moments of conversion. Like Peter, I rise and fall like a see-saw in my faith. But Jesus is always there, calling me to "Come," urging me to trust him, to love him, and to feed his sheep (Matt. 14:29 and John 21:15–17).

Each moment of conversion to little things (like trusting the process just a bit more) is also a moment of conversion to that big thing: loving God and neighbor more deeply. Like the servants in another parable, I hope that by being faithful in little things, my Lord will give me the grace to be faithful also in much.[2] Someday, I want to hear not, "O you of little faith, why did you doubt?" but "Well done, good and trustworthy servant; you have been trustworthy in a few things, I will put you in charge of many things; enter into the joy of your Lord" (Matt. 25:21, 23, NRSV, adapted). In my reading of this verse, to be put in charge of many things is not tied to earthly power or authority, but deeper servanthood, more faithful discipleship, a fuller conversion. And to enter into the joy of the Lord is to be converted to a greater participation in God's life.

Conversion ultimately means desiring "to restore all people to unity with God and each other in Christ," that is, to fulfill the mission of the universal church and to live more fully into the Great Commandment (Catechism, *BCP* 855; Luke 10:27). Through faith in Christ, we are drawn more deeply into God's own life. The mission of the church at its core is a call to participation in the very lovelife of God.

This vision of conversion as participation in the lovelife of the Holy Trinity is behind my theology of discernment and fuels my desire to be in deeper community with the discernment process. Discernment is, after all, a gift of the Holy Spirit. Discernment involves participating in the Trinity's life through listening to the Holy Spirit. Listening is an activity of our whole being—heart, soul, mind, and body—and our deepest discernment is a form of worshiping the Holy Spirit.

When I listen to some people talk about what the process does they use words like "interview" and "screening." But discernment is not primarily an interviewing process, even a prayerful one. As Suzanne Farnham, executive director of the Christian Vocation Project, writes, "Spiritual discernment is not synonymous with what might be described as prayerful Christian decision making. It is that and something more—something much deeper."[3] What is that "something much deeper"? I think Barbara Brown Taylor gets at the heart of this "something" when she writes:

Even now, some Christians have trouble listening to God. Many of us prefer to speak. Our corporate prayers are punctuated with phrases

such as "Hear us, Lord" or "Lord, hear our prayer," as if the burden
to listen were on God and not us. We name our concerns, giving God
suggestions on what to do about them. What reversal of power might
occur if we turned the process around, naming our concerns and
asking God to tell us what to do about them? "Speak, Lord, for your
servants are listening."

Sometimes I think we do all the talking because we are afraid God
won't. Or, conversely, that God will. Either way, staying preoccupied
with our own words seems a safer bet than opening ourselves up either
to God's silence or God's speech, both of which have the power to
undo us.[4]

What reversal of power might occur if we turned the *discernment* process
around, people "in process" and "the process" together in one community
naming our concerns and asking the Holy Spirit to tell us what to do about
them? Are we praying, as Samuel did, "Speak, Lord, for your servant is listening" (1 Sam. 3:10, NASB, adapted)? Or are we only talking to ourselves?

Some people I've talked with have argued that the nuts and bolts of discernment happen best on the parish (and later, seminary) level. They say that
the discernment process on the diocesan level should simply sift through,
weigh, and come to consensus using the materials that the person in process
and that parish-level discerners provide. Commissions on Ministry have neither the time nor the energy to engage in the sort of "community building"
I propose. Certainly, this is a common view of how the process should work,
but while this division of labor is theoretically efficient, I am not convinced
it is the best way to be discerning. I agree that it's unreasonable to expect a
Commission on Ministry to do the bulk of the "nuts-and-bolts" discernment.
But to remain distant, as most GenX folks in process perceive most Commissions on Ministry, is not an option if a Commission on Ministry wants
to be more than a bureaucracy of prayerful Christian decision makers, however efficient.

To discern is to listen to the Holy Spirit. To listen is to worship the Holy
Spirit. To worship is to participate with each other in the lovelife of the Trinity
through the Holy Spirit. To participate is to be in communion with the Trinity
and each other in the Holy Spirit. To be in communion is to be in community with the Trinity and each other in the Holy Spirit. And to be in community is to live together in the everyday realities of human existence, where
Christ met us when he became flesh and lived among us (John 1:14). As the
Greek fathers of the church said of Christ, "The divinity became human so
that humanity might become divine."

But while we already participate in the divine community of the Holy Trinity in the here and now, it's important not to idealize community. We all know that the church on earth is imperfect. And while the Trinity is perfect, that does not mean that if we participate in the lovelife of the Holy Trinity more deeply, we will be removed from all suffering. After all, we worship a Father who grieves, a Son who still bears the wounds of an unjust execution, and a Spirit who "intercedes for us with groanings too deep for words" (Rom. 8:26, NASB). When I write about "community," therefore, I do not mean some frictionless utopia. Community is a dynamic life, not a static state, and until Christ is "all, and in all" (Col. 3:11, NASB), our communities of discernment will have their ups and downs, just like a see-saw. But that is no excuse for leaving things as they are.

DESCRIBING THE SPECK: JESUS' CALL TO COMMUNITY

Jesus says that once I've begun to remove the log from my eye, I will begin to see the speck in my sibling's eye more clearly. Maybe I should, as my friends have often advised, "leave well enough alone." "Just get through it," they say. Yet one of the signs of an authentic call may be a sense of restlessness, of dissatisfaction with things as they are; to ignore these feelings might very well be to ignore the movement of the Spirit.[5] The naked truth is that I feel compelled to try to describe the speck as I see it, because if I don't, I believe I will be unfaithful to myself, to my neighbor, and to God.

I'm taking a risk here, because I know there's a possibility that some involved in the discernment process may be offended. Some may not even feel there is a speck in the process's eye. But I've decided to trust that those who have taken on the difficult task of serving on Commissions on Ministry and in other roles related to the discernment process on every level are willing to take a risk, too: to try to love, accept, and trust me as I have decided to try to love, accept, and trust those who are involved in my own process.

With the log coming out of my eye, I am now beginning to care about the discernment process as a community and as a vital ministry of the church, rather than caring only about "just getting through" the process. I will share my deepest feelings, both positive and negative, in the hope that those whose ministry includes the selection and formation of this church's future clergy might find in these feelings "anything true . . . anything good." If any decide to "think on these things" (Phil. 4:8), I hope those so moved will respond in kind, with their own deepest feelings, both positive and negative, and that we can enter into a mutually converting conversation that includes the whole church.

Here, then, is the speck as I see it: I have often felt that the discernment process is controlled by strangers who do not know me. At best, I feel the process can know *about* me, but cannot *know* me. I thus feel left out of the very community of discernment I have sought, and I suspect that there are others out there, especially Xers, who feel similarly.

The way I just described this speck reflects my own assumption that community is a necessary precondition for authoritative discernment of a Christian vocation, lay or ordained. It also assumes that while I believe a community of discernment exists within the process as it is now structured, not including those "in process" as active participants within that community makes listening for the voice of the Holy Spirit more difficult for all involved. Discernment is more likely to be done in the right spirit (i.e., *the* Spirit) if approached as a consultation of the Holy Spirit by those "in process" and "the process" together, rather than as an evaluation of those "in process" by "the process," with the assumption that the Spirit will work everything out for the greater glory of God, even when the process errs. "All things work together for good for those who love God" (Rom. 8:28, NRSV), but this does not excuse us from community. For discernment to be both challenging and joyful, I believe we need to be present and known to each other in an atmosphere of mutual hospitality and accountability on both the diocesan and the parish level.

My assumptions are rooted in the very core of my emotional and intellectual being; they're not simply gut instinct or rational theory, but both. My instinct is rooted in my generational identity, and my theory is rooted in my religious identity—and vice versa. As an Xer, I locate authority within community because it is through community that I know and am known by my sisters and brothers, in the fullness of life, not only when we are at our best or worst, but everywhere in between. Thus, when I am confronted or challenged or even complimented by a member of my community, I am more likely to receive it as authoritative than if it comes from a stranger. As a Christian I locate authority within the Trinity, because the community of the church participates in the community of the Holy Trinity through the body of Christ, the source of the church's life. Thus, I expect *every* ministry of the church, by grace, to strive toward becoming more fully a community in the Trinity's life, especially those ministries of the church (both diocesan and parish level) whose call is to raise up servant-leaders for our communities of faith (whether lay or ordained).

When the process did not live up to these theological and generational expectations, I felt left outside my own community. And so, without even fully realizing it—at first perhaps without realizing it consciously at all—I expected an invitation from those who were in charge of the process to join the community of discernment I assumed must exist as a precondition to discernment. I looked for that invitation, but whether my log was even more blinding than I thought, or the invitation got lost in the mail, or the community of discernment I sought on the diocesan level didn't exist after all, I never received it.

I felt that what I received instead were several directives from on high, from people I didn't know and whose place and authority in my life I couldn't quite figure out—emotionally speaking, if not intellectually. I was told to show up or not to show up at certain meetings, to turn in certain forms, to write certain essays, to make sure others submitted certain reports about me. Each deadline, rather than drawing me closer into the community of discernment I sought, seemed to distance me from it. I'm sure that was not the intention of all these meetings, forms, essays, and reports. I think all these things were intended to get to know me better, but I felt they only skimmed the surface.

Rationally, I knew that the instructions I received were legitimate, because this was the official way priests are selected and formed in the Episcopal Church. But emotionally I felt alienated, patronized, perhaps in all the bureaucracy a bit dehumanized. When I was not given the opportunity firsthand to share my own experience or to get to know the people who were making important decisions affecting the course of my life, I felt shut out. When I was told these decisions were "for your own good," I felt that the process put me back into the very parent-child relationship from which, as a young adult, I had just emerged; it felt like a step backward in development, not an encouragement to take steps forward. When I found that applying for postulancy was more tied up with red tape than doing my taxes, I felt that the impersonal bureaucracy was jarringly inconsistent with the promise in the Baptismal Covenant to respect the dignity of every human being (*BCP* 304–5).

These are strong words, strong feelings. A lot of these feelings were reactions to perceptions that may or may not have been accurate. But they do call into question some of the methods employed in the process. I'm as sure now as I was then that nobody was trying to be rude or insensitive—in fact, quite the opposite. But no matter how often they apologized for the way things "had" to be done, explaining very calmly and rationally why they did things the way they did, still in my gut I felt there must be a better way.

I now recognize that part of my desire for an invitation was for an opening through which I could control my own fate. I wanted to preempt not only the process's power, but God's as well. My control issue was, after all, rooted in my mistrust of the process to begin with. But my desire for an invitation was also a sincere yearning for community with others in the Holy Spirit. I wanted to experience the discernment process as a ministry of the church rather than as something I just needed "to get through."

So to the process I would like to say: I don't blame you (now) for not sending the invitation I looked for, because I now believe that this community of discernment is actually a surprise party God has decided to throw for *us*, not a party you were supposed to throw for me or I for you. How egotistical and self-centered I've been when I look back. But now, looking forward, I believe that we are cordially invited by God to deepen our participation in that community of which we are already a part, but that will be enhanced, I hope, by a fuller participation of all my GenX peers desiring to come. We're too big now for the kids' table at Thanksgiving. In a spirit of hospitality, it's time to make a place for us next to you at the table of the Great Thanksgiving.

REMOVING THE SPECK: A VISION OF COMMUNITY

Jesus said that once we saw more clearly, we could assist our sibling in removing that speck. Once I began to trust the process, or rather, decided to trust that God would work through the people in charge of the process just as God had worked through me, I began to empathize with the people, rather than to blame the process. For instance, I talked with some friends who are both GenX priests and Commission on Ministry members. Their position between these two worlds gives them a unique perspective. Because they are Commission on Ministry members, they know the joys and tribulations of that ministry. Because they are Xers, they empathize with young people in the process. Because they are both, I believe they are trustworthy witnesses (Heb. 12:1).

I asked these "GenX/COMers" why aspirants (and those at other stages of the process as well) are not included more as participants in the commission side of the process. One priest's answer was particularly succinct. She told me her diocese used to have retreats with commission members and aspirants, but the retreats only made their task all the more difficult. Imagine getting to know and like a person but not discerning that they have a call to the priestly vocation. It becomes extremely difficult to say no to that person, even though that's part of the Commission on Ministry's mission. Commission on Ministry members go through an extraordinary amount of heart wrenching and soul searching as it is. The last thing they want to do is say no to a friend. So, in order to maintain professional objectivity, commission members have had to set the boundaries farther away than they would like. She conceded that this makes it difficult to know the aspirant, as opposed only to knowing *about* the aspirant through a manila file. One of the dangers, then, from the

Commission on Ministry side, is that the process may become too subjective. We are all humans, after all, and perfect objectivity is never possible, especially when it comes to questions of call and vocation, gifts and ministry. But is it more important to be in relationship or to be in control?

From my perspective, I fear more that the Commission on Ministry will be too objective, that in the universally human desire to be in control they will not take into account the movement of the Spirit, who has been known to do some pretty loopy things. Our salvation history is one counterintuitive story after another: an old couple past childbearing years told by God to leave their hometown and to go to some distant promised land, with God all the while reassuring them that they will be the progenitors of a great people, more numerous than the sand of the sea or the stars of the sky. It's a laughable proposition, and Sarah does laugh (Gen. 18:12–15). Then there's Moses—a stuttering murderer who becomes Israel's liberator and lawgiver (contradictory roles when you think about them). And let's not forget Jesus. He didn't have much life experience, but he sure suffered a lot for such a young person. As for the question of "call," I've often heard the cynical remark that if the twelve disciples went in front of the average Commission on Ministry, the disciple most likely to be granted postulancy would be Judas Iscariot—he was, after all, the treasurer (John 13:29).

While some people's tendency may be to protect the objectivity of the process, the Spirit's desire may be to inject some subjectivity into the process. But would making the discernment process even more subjective than it already is make the community any more discerning? Possibly, but not necessarily—perhaps not even probably. The question of how to invite the Spirit to deepen both the process's community and its discernment comes down to practicality: How do we make sure the process is neither too subjective nor too objective? How do we discern the right balance?

The Eastern Orthodox have a saying, "Let your mind descend into your heart," and this question of balance has descended to the bottom of my heart ever since I first began to listen to the Spirit calling me to ordained ministry.[6] I began to discern that call, in fact, while living in a Benedictine monastery for a summer between my sophomore and junior years in college. It was there that I began to learn the art of *lectio divina*, "sacred reading," a form of silent meditation on a word or phrase of scripture practiced by monks throughout the millennia.

I have often meditated on two simple phrases of scripture: 1 Thessalonians 5:19, "Do not quench the Spirit," and 1 John 4:1b, "Test the spirits" (NASB). I've always paired these two verses in my *lectio divina*, because they are so complementary. Together they offer an understanding of discernment as a grace-filled balancing act between "testing the spirits" on the one hand, while being careful not to "quench the Spirit" on the other.

I began this essay by stating that I sensed an imbalance in the way I relate to the process, and perhaps also in the way the process relates to me. It feels like I'm on a see-saw, and that something's wrong. But when I meditate on these verses, I discover the balance I've sought. Together, I believe they offer a way of balancing the objective and the subjective, thereby showing a way forward to a deeper experience of discernment and community in our church, both for those in process and for those charged with the ministry of the process.

As I've alluded, the simplest way I have found to imagine this balance is to picture the basic schoolyard see-saw. Imagine two kids riding that see-saw: the one kid is objectivity and the other is subjectivity. The fulcrum—the point on the see-saw where it's balanced—I call "interjectivity."

As a kid, I remember trying to remain at that place of balance when playing on the see-saw with my sister, Anna. Each of us would try to adjust how much weight we brought to bear on our end until, miraculously, we found ourselves floating, perfectly balanced. This only lasted a little while, of course, because the slightest movement on either end would snap the toy back into action, and the game of finding the right balance would begin again.

My concept of community is very much like the game of finding balance on a see-saw. But just as on a see-saw, community is never a static state. Community is always being influenced by the position of one end relative to the other, and will pass through that place of balance every time one end goes up and the other end comes down. The goal, then, is not so much to weld the see-saw of community into that place of balance—that would ruin the toy and make for a pretty boring time—but to recognize and foster those moments when the see-saw is in balance, because those are particularly Spirit-filled moments. It's also important to recognize that these Spirit-filled moments of balance would not exist without the constant dynamic interrelationship between the objective and the subjective. If one kid on the see-saw decided to go home, the other kid would find herself sitting in the dust. It's impossible to play on the see-saw when there's only one.

Imagine the process as being on the objective side of the see-saw and a person in process on the subjective side (or vice versa). If we look at this game as a competition to see which "kid" can get to the top and which "kid" can leave the other in the dust, we get nowhere fast. So, too, if the kid on the one side weighs a thousand pounds and the kid on the other weighs a hundred, the heavy one would be able to get the lighter one into the air, but that's it. The lighter one wouldn't be able to nudge the heavier one off the ground, unless she stood up on the seat and suddenly jumped in the air and back onto the seat; but that's a very dangerous thing to do. But if the two sides cooperate, enter into a mutual relationship in which each actively helps the other find that place of balance, we begin to get a picture of the community of discernment for which I yearn.

My vision of community, then, is an intentionally playful one. I invite the church to play around with this toy and see what we can come up with; to get us started, I've come up with the following (hardly complete) list.[7] Imagine this list as raw materials—like popsicle sticks, glue, rubber bands, toothpicks, and so on—for building a miniature see-saw. I hope that by looking at the different "weights" (that is, emphases) we place on either end of the see-saw, we can begin to see how they interact to foster—or to squelch—those Spirit-filled moments of balance.

To certain people playing with this toy, some characteristics may seem good and others bad. But are "rational" or "emotional" good characteristics or bad ones? Like these two, many characteristics can be taken either way depending on context. It's possible, perhaps even desirable, for a community to contain two seemingly opposite elements in order to attain balance.[8]

The Subjective at its extreme may fail to test the spirits and tends toward:	The Interjective at its most balanced tests without quenching and tends toward:	The Objective at its extreme may quench the Spirit and tends toward:
Democracy	Community	Bureaucracy
Irrational	Transrational	Rational
Emotional	Transemotional	Unemotional
Immanent God	Trinity	Transcendent God
Personal	Responsible/reciprocal	Impersonal
Participant	Participant-observer	Observer
Personal qualities	Call first, gifts second	Professional qualifications
Inclusive	Mutual hospitality	Exclusive
Consensus of people	Sense of the Spirit	Vote of members
Flexible/disorderly	Flexible yet orderly	Inflexible/orderly
Egalitarian	Authoritative	Authoritarian
Rushes through	As long/short as it takes	Drags along

I present this list as a way of questioning our assumptions about discernment, the Spirit, the process, and each other. On its own, the list won't answer the question of how we can be in right relationship with each other in the process, but creatively fiddling with it, expanding upon it, and looking at it from different angles just might point the way. The point is not to overanalyze this list or to use it to diagnose others' problems, but to play with it. It's a toy, not a diagnostic tool. If we treat it as a tool, we will soon find ourselves trying to tighten a metric bolt with an English wrench, and a toy wrench at that.

I could go on to explain in excruciating detail how to play with this toy so that we build the perfect discernment process. But I remember as a child—which wasn't that long ago, as I'm often reminded by my Boomer friends—being very impatient with my father as he explained how to work a model-train set. "I can do it for myself," I remember thinking—even if that turned out later not to be true. In this case, however, I trust we're all smart enough to play with this toy constructively. But please, play nice. And don't break it. Share it with others, especially those in process, and include us in your reindeer games. Use the toy to stimulate questions on all levels, not primarily about how the process could be better structured, but about how we in the process could be better relationed, not only to each other, but to the Holy Trinity.

LOGJAMS AND SAWMILLS: SEEING THE FOREST FOR THE TREES

After I had been delayed for the second time in my own discernment process due to issues related to my youth, Suzanne Farnham offered to assemble a Listening Hearts Discernment Group for me. She asked three people I'd never met to discern with me the next step in my pilgrimage of faith and ministry. It was one of the most powerful experiences of community in the life of the Spirit I have ever had.

One of the principles of this way of discernment is an emphasis on images as signs of the Spirit. At our final meeting (which we didn't know would be our final one until the following happened), I saw an image of a logjam. I thought at first that the logjammed river I saw was the Episcopal Church, but then I realized it was an image of my life within the church. Something was jamming up my flow in the Spirit, and I was later able to identify that logjam with mistrust. The group then asked me: What tools can you use to pry loose that logjam? The association with Jesus' image of the log and the speck was not difficult after that.

That image helped get the river of my life within the church flowing again, and this essay is one of its fruits. I offer this essay to the larger church because I sense I'm not the only one with these questions and concerns, so in a sense the river is the Episcopal Church, or perhaps the Spirit within the church. In order for us to begin to extract these logs out of the river (and our eyes) and send them to the sawmill, we must be clear about the central questions facing the church concerning the discernment process. Otherwise, we won't see the forest for the trees.

The solution is not to clear-cut the forest. But we do need to cut down the termite-infested trees and those whose growth prevents the saplings from soaking up the sunshine of God's love. These trees are not people; no person needs to be cut down. Rather, these trees are the things in our lives that keep us from deeper, more loving, trusting, and open relationships with each other and God. If the discernment process on all levels, especially the diocesan, cannot model these relationships for those in its process, how can the process expect potential ordained and lay ministers to model these relationships for others?

So the central question this essay boils down to is: What is the right relationship between a person in process and the discernment process, especially on the diocesan level, that will most effectively discern what the Spirit is saying to the church (Rev. 2–3)? I believe that any relationship between "the process" and those "in process" that is intentional about being interjective *and that includes those in process in shaping its common life* will begin to find the answer. This "answer" will not be a static solution to a mystery but our very participation in that mystery.

It's not good enough just to know about *each* other. I cannot trust the process unless I know the people who make up the process. They cannot trust me unless they know me. Otherwise, even this essay, which is an attempt to establish that trust, might be looked upon as a threat to the authority of the process. Without a relationship, this entire essay is presumptuous; without a relationship, the entire process is presumptuous.

My fear is, if a mere aspirant writes an essay, will anyone listen? If a tree, or in this case, a sapling, falls in the forest and nobody is around, will it make a sound? I have tried to express my own vision of the right relationship between those in process and those in charge of the process based on my own struggle to "trust the process." But through this vision, I pray not that God will convert the process to suit me, but that I will be converted to suit God, and through God, we will both be converted to suit each other. This is my prayer for the discernment process, and it is my prayer for the whole church as well, as we struggle with those crises of communion that can be resolved only through discernment in community. For ultimately, this issue is larger than aspirants and Commissions on Ministry, larger than logs and specks. It's about the future of our church.

NOTES

1. Mitch Albom, *Tuesdays with Morrie: An Old Man, a Young Man, and the Last Great Lesson* (New York: Doubleday, 1997), 151.
2. See both Matthew 25:14–30 and Luke 19:11–27. The Matthean version raises the question for me of whether the process is being faithful with the

"talents" of the young people entrusted it; the standard operating procedure of having us wait might be like burying the talent. But the Lukan version raises the question of whether Xers aren't in fact expecting that the "kingdom of God should immediately appear" (Luke 19:11, KJV). That is, are we Xers being too impatient?

3. Suzanne Farnham, "Beyond Prayerful Analysis," *Explorations: The Newsletter of the Christian Vocation Project, Inc.* vol. 9, no. 1 (winter 1999).

4. Barbara Brown Taylor, *When God Is Silent* (Cambridge, Mass.: Cowley Publications, 1998), 50–51. Presented originally as the 1997 Lyman Beecher Lectures on Preaching, Yale Divinity School.

5. See Suzanne G. Farnham et al., *Listening Hearts: Discerning Call in Community* (Harrisburg, Pa.: Morehouse Publishing, 1991), 11.

6. Ibid., 2.

7. This list, of course, is deceptively schematic. For although it presents the qualities of each category on a continuum, as if the proper balance between the subjective and the objective were merely a matter of finding the midpoint between the two, in fact each characteristic affects and is affected by the others. So, for instance, if a community emphasizes the rational, this emphasis will be influenced by all the other characteristics, such as how democratic and hospitable that community is; conversely, democracy and hospitality will be affected by rationality, and so forth. The basic assumptions behind this approach are based on "systems thinking," outlined in *Generation to Generation: Family Process in Church and Synagogue* by Rabbi Edwin H. Friedman (New York: The Guildford Press, 1985), 14–19.

8. Three items in the middle column, "transrational," "transemotional," and "call first, gifts second," deserve explaining. I have borrowed the term *transrational* from the late Orthodox theologian Alexander Schmemann (see *For the Life of the World* [Crestwood, N.Y.: St. Vladimir's Seminary Press, 1963], 104). It refers, essentially, to faith, a mystery that is not irrational (though it is "foolishness to Gentiles," 1 Cor. 1:18–25) but that is not capable of being explained entirely by reason, either. It transcends both categories; hence it is transrational. An apologetics that accepts the rationalism of the Enlightenment, therefore, may be more likely to do damage to faith than uphold it; *transrational* is a category fit for the apologetics of the postmodern era.

So, too, something can be *transemotional*, that is, a mystery (such as love), which is neither purely emotional nor capable of being dissected unemotionally. Transrational and transemotional things, such as faith, hope, and love, can be thought about and deeply felt, but they ultimately go beyond the limits of rationality and emotion. They are greater than our human capacities to comprehend them because their being is in God, who cannot be comprehended (literally, "surrounded").

Finally, I list "call first, gifts second" as the balance between "personal qualities" and "personal qualifications." This reflects my bias that we are all, by virtue of our baptism, called to ministry. Our call to ministry is irrespective of our particular gifts; in fact, God may call us to a ministry at any point in our lives for which we are eminently *unqualified*. If we do the task of discernment while looking primarily at a person's gifts, or personal, objective qualifications, we may miss the specific nature of the Spirit's call to ministry for that person. For example, a stockbroker may be called by the Spirit to teach first-grade Sunday School, not to be parish treasurer, although if we went by qualifications that would be counterintuitive. Sometimes it's the first-grade teacher whom God calls to be the treasurer. At the other extreme, personal qualities (such as affability, humor, etc.) do not determine whether a person has a call, either. "He has a lovely way about him" does not mean he's called to preside at the Eucharist, even though he'd look great doing it.

SECTION
TWO

FORMATION
AND MINISTRY

A Call for Curacy

Following a Residency Model by Getting Congregations
Involved as "Teaching Parishes"

Benjamin A. Shambaugh

TAKING A RISK

When St. John's Episcopal Church in Olney, Maryland, decided to increase
its staff by calling a twenty-nine-year-old, just-graduated deacon to work part-
time for the parish and part-time for the parish's Episcopal day school, a question immediately arose: what should this new clergyperson's title be? While
"religion teacher" and "chaplain" fit the expectations from the school, and
"youth minister" fit those from the church, none of the names seemed like
they'd be attractive to senior seminarians. As a result, the church bestowed
the rather vague title of "assistant rector" on a priest whose ministry of religion teacher/chaplain/youth minister allowed little real time to "assist the
rector" with anything, much less to learn what being a parish priest is all
about! This comment is not meant to denigrate the vital responsibilities of
chaplain or youth minister. It is, instead, an example of the need for clarity
in the calling of young clergy, as well as a proposal for a different role for the
newly ordained: that of a curate.

A *curate* is usually defined simply as a clergyperson assisting a priest in
charge of a congregation. The word *curate* is derived from the Latin word *cure*,
which means "spiritual care; the care of souls." That, in itself, defines well the
role to which most clergy feel called. Modern French has maintained this sense
by calling a parish priest a *curé*, perhaps a more elegant term than the
American version, pastor. In this essay, *curate* will refer to a newly ordained
person in a ministry specifically designed both to serve a congregation and
to further his or her preparation for service to the wider church. This type of
curacy is roughly equivalent to a medical residency—a time when, under
supervision, a newly ordained person is given the tools and experience to grow
into the fullness of sacerdotal ministry and thereby to discover what it means
to be responsible for a "cure of souls."

Episcopal seminaries convince seminarians that with the dreaded GOEs (General Ordination Exams) under their belts, they are at the cutting edge of ministry. But the cutting edge is often light years away from the struggles of parish life and the questions of organizational development, youth ministry, education, volunteer recruitment, stewardship, and fund-raising that most parishes face. How many seminarians graduate having learned fund accounting or management of budgets, much less the intricacies of management of volunteers or staff who are Christian everywhere but in church? Seminaries expect students will learn these things once in a parish, and parishes assume their priests have already learned these things in seminary! While mentoring relationships, colleague groups, and intentional practical programs within seminaries would be a great help with these issues, I call on the church to take the risk and make the investment necessary to provide a first experience of ordained ministry that is positive and productive for the newly ordained person and the parish. Curacies, ministries that purposefully cycle new clergy through the many aspects of ministry in a parish, are an excellent way to offer practical training.

THE ROLE OF A MENTOR AND PARISH

Practical training really happens when a more senior clergyperson is willing to take time to serve the curate as a mentor. In my first parish, I was the fourth clergyperson on the staff and was able to benefit from the mentoring of the rector and the other clergy. In my second parish, I was the second clergyperson on the staff but was blessed over time by close relationships with two cathedral deans and with three bishops of the Convocation of American Episcopal Churches in Europe, whose office was just upstairs from mine. In his own way, each of these mentors became a sounding board, a model, a teacher, and a friend. They offered reality checks and reminders, often recounting stories from many long years of experience, reminding me again and again of the humanness of our church and the power of the Holy Spirit to work in and through it. Because of them, I later could greet the struggles I faced as a new rector, thinking, "So this is what they were talking about," while still retaining a confidence, based on their experience, that "this too shall pass."

If the rector or senior clergyperson is unable or unwilling to serve the curate in this mentoring role, it may be best taken by another clergyperson, by a curate support committee, or even by the parish itself. In the latter situation, a remarkable paradigm shift occurs. Rather than being apprenticed to the rector (or bishop), the curate becomes apprenticed to the community of faith—the congregation. Just this sort of shift has occurred in the medical community. While in the past medical residencies and internships were essentially the responsibility of one senior physician, they are now the responsibility of entire hospitals. When the hospital took over, residents were better able to experience a wide spectrum of medical practice, while avoiding some of the hazing and master/servant relationships that accompanied the intern or residency experience of past generations. Hospitals that follow this model define themselves as "teaching hospitals."

Hopefully, congregations that take on curates will follow suit and begin to see themselves as "teaching parishes." To avoid the overwork and the often unintentional hazing that is also common with clergy, parishes called to this teaching role will need to become practitioners of clergy wellness and clergy care. This focus could well have a ripple effect throughout the entire congregation, possibly even transforming the image of the church as a "hospital for sinners" to a community of caring that emphasizes wellness and health for the whole household of faith.

POSSIBLE OBJECTIONS TO CURACIES AND RESPONSES TO THE OBJECTIONS

Congregations considering becoming "teaching parishes" and hiring a curate might have concerns, including the following:

> Specific needs: "Rather than a jack-of-all-trades who dabbles in everything, we need a youth minister or someone to assist our burned-out rector."

Most parishes in the Episcopal Church are in desperate need of a revitalized youth ministry. A successful youth ministry attracts new families and builds the church of tomorrow, even while it builds up the church of today. A youth minister can be a great asset in making this happen. Unfortunately, chronological youth does not a youth minister make; neither does ordination. A young ordained person may have the skills necessary for this kind of work; by and large, though, seminaries train their students to be rectors, not youth ministers. A curacy, which may include youth ministry among many other facets, better augments seminary education. Parishes that really want a youth minister should hire one, lay or ordained. Parishes that want a priest who "does youth" but is capable and trained for more may opt for a curate instead. In this case, it is important for expectations on both sides to be as clear and as well-defined as possible.

> Cost: "An ordained person costs a lot. Are we getting our money's worth out of someone who is so young and inexperienced?"

Unfortunately, as escalating costs of salary, housing, and benefits have combined with increased financial needs (because of student loans and the high cost of seminary) and the ever-higher average age (and correspondingly larger financial and family responsibilities) of seminarians, the cost of hiring a curate has become proportionally higher than in previous years. Compensation for other clergy and parish staff has risen as well. For example, a study of my own parish's budgets over the past ten years shows that money spent on program line items has not changed significantly, but the cost of salaries and benefits has more than doubled! Even with this increase, though, several staff members are still compensated at or under minimum levels suggested by diocesan guidelines. This sort of underpaying or underbenefiting of staff is, unfortunately, a common occurrence, as evidenced by an Internet survey that raised the question of just compensation to all Episcopal clergy under thirty-five. Interestingly, while the respondents unanimously felt underpaid and undercompensated, many also recognized that their hiring represented a "leap of faith" for their financially strapped congregations. The bottom line is that clergy pay and benefits are expensive—often too expensive for parishes who would otherwise love to have another person on staff. As a result, newly ordained clergy often find themselves hired as vicars of missions, college chaplains, youth ministers, and the like. Because the academic demands of seminary leave little time for practical training in subjects that would be helpful in these areas, new clergy in these positions frequently find themselves feeling overwhelmed, isolated, demoralized, and cynical after only a few years of ordained ministry.

It is important to note that because most diocesan pay scales are geared to years of service, curates are among the least expensive of clergy, in some places costing as little as half as much as their rectors. Furthermore, while the financial cost of hiring another clergyperson (even a young, newly ordained one) is large, so too are the potential benefits. Church-growth studies have shown that in order to grow from pastoral to program size, most parishes need additional ordained staff. Having a young person in this role tends to attract others in the same age bracket—the very group that is most lacking in our churches. The parish that spends part of its endowment on a curate will probably reap a greater return on that investment than on the highest-performing stock. Endowments, after all, are for securing the ability of a parish to preach the gospel and thereby further the mission of the church. Conventional wisdom and prudent financial strategies say that a parish should save its endowment to maintain stability, counting on the "miracle of compound interest." I advocate a somewhat riskier approach. Investing endowment funds in younger clergy may bring about an even more significant miracle—the miracle of compound growth in mission and ministry.

Such an approach may upset the more level-headed, who have the "best interest" of the church at heart. But the best interest of the church isn't necessarily 9.25 percent per annum! The problem with a maintenance strategy is that it fails to bring in more people. We all know beautiful Episcopal churches with healthy endowments and few people in attendance on Sunday. These stand in stark contrast to evangelical megachurches that have no endowments and very simple buildings but invest instead in staff and have huge congregations. Certainly one can do mission without mammon, but ironically, we've gotten so caught up in storing up treasure for tomorrow that we run the risk of dying as a denomination before ever getting the chance to use it. One of our best hopes for avoiding such a fate is the adoption of radical but potentially high-yield mission strategies, such as the renewal of the curacy.

By sharing a curacy with a neighboring Episcopal parish, an Episcopal school, or a Lutheran (or other denominational) parish, a church might find the "critical mass" of needed funding. In certain cases, diocesan or parish funds specifically designated for outreach or theological education might also be tapped. Training and preparation of newly ordained clergy is an outreach both to the church and to the larger community as well. Paying for curates with diocesan or bishop's discretionary funds isn't done much anymore, but the perspective of "curacy as outreach" may also loosen up money designated from these areas as well.

Longevity: "Why should we go through all this building up of relationship to lose someone after only three years?"

For the person in the pew, most likely the biggest issue in hiring a curate is longevity. A curate, involved in all aspects of the parish, naturally tends to develop significant relationships with church members, many of whom—especially youth—can go through considerable grief upon the curate's departure. Rapid change in leadership can be devastating to the most successful of youth programs. However, when parishioners take ownership in their part of educating, forming, and preparing their curate for ministry in the wider church, much of that pain can be transformed into pride.

Unlike medicine, in which issues are relatively discrete and a resident can be exposed to various aspects of medicine in a short period of time, parish ministry, for the most part, is much less defined and much more relationship-based. As a result, a series of brief rotations in particular areas would probably not work as well for a curate as would taking on several different areas of ministry for, say, a day or a half-day each week over a period of several years. This sort of program would allow time for needed trust to develop. Exceptions to this might include more distinct areas of ministry such as advanced Clinical Pastoral Education, prison ministry, hospice, crisis intervention, conference organization, or educational programs that could be effectively handled in a residency-like rotation.

From the curate's perspective, a clear definition of this "period of several years" is extremely helpful. If curacies are set for a specific period of time (say three or five years), the curate need not be anxious about what will happen next. At the end of the specified period, it will be time to move on. Because the parish sees this as part of its ministry, the curate will be supported during the search for the next position, rather than having to prepare secretively to leave.

> Ordination status: "Why invest so much time and money in a curate
> who, for the first half of his or her ministry with us, will not even be
> able to function as a priest?"

From a rector's perspective, concern about hiring a curate is not as likely to be about salary or tenure as about ordination status. As much as we celebrate the theology of the diaconate, the reality is that most rectors want a second priest, not a deacon. Rather than raising up diaconal ministry, parishes who call graduating seminarians often find themselves feeling cheated and increasingly frustrated while they wait six months to a year before getting what they need—and feel they are paying for! One way of solving this problem is to follow the model of Roman Catholic dioceses that ordain seminarians to the diaconate the summer before their final year of seminary, thus allowing their last (in our case, third) year of seminary and seminary fieldwork to be a "diaconal year." If deacons were placed in fieldwork parishes that could not normally afford curacies, this combination of "diaconal" and "senior" year would increase the visibility of the diaconate in the wider church. It would also allow the seminarian greater fieldwork experience and opportunity for reflection and discernment during the last year of being supported by the seminary community. In reality, fieldwork parishes frequently have their seminarians fill diaconal roles, liturgically and otherwise, thus treating them like clergy. Many seminarians enhance this perspective by wearing clerical collars with so-called seminarian stripes. Ordaining seminarians to the diaconate prior to their senior (or intern) year would both legitimize these roles and provide real assistance to overburdened clergy of small and rural parishes. A diaconal senior year would also decrease the perspective that the diaconate is a "stepping-stone" to the priesthood, thus highlighting the ministry of those called to the permanent diaconate. Most significant, a diaconal senior year would allow parishes the immediate benefit of calling curates who are also priests.

CONCLUSION

The renewal of the curacy would entail a certain degree of risk-taking on the part of congregations, but the potential benefits far outweigh the costs. Creative solutions are available for funding and supporting curates, and parishes that find themselves in danger of dying might consider this proposal as a way to infuse their congregations with a new sense of mission and life.

For young priests, curacies present the advantage of a formal system of support and mentoring from fellow clergy and from the community of the baptized, who, after all, represent the first order of ministry. By claiming the responsibilities and joys of raising up new leadership, the laity will reclaim for themselves a sense of ownership often lacking in priest-centered, "Father knows best" parishes. Young curates would also have the opportunity to experience systematically a broad range of ministries, rather than being required to specialize in a particular area in which they may have little interest or skill.

In short, by following a model based on a medical residency, perhaps combined with the ordination of seminarians to the diaconate in their final year, curacies offer a practical, mission-oriented way of providing for new clergy while simultaneously reinvigorating our churches.

Youth's Authority

A Spiritual Revolution

Margaret K. Schwarzer

A few days before I was ordained to the diaconate, an Episcopal priest in his fifties pulled me aside and gave me some advice. He said that, like me, he had looked even younger than he was when he had begun his ordained ministry, and he had learned a lot about the challenges of being a young leader in the church as a result of his boyish features. He explained that developing a successful ministry would require me to be prepared for other people's shock at my youthful appearance. When I recognized their discomfort, he suggested that I offer them a good, crisp summary of where my authority lay. Then he whispered the line that had been given to him when he was ordained some twenty years before.

Seven months later, when the first gray-haired father of the bride peered into my face with obvious distress over the fact that a young woman would be presiding at the marriage of his daughter, I was prepared. "Exactly how old are you?" he demanded, with a bit of bravado overlaying his anxiety. I looked him straight in the eye and matched the strength of my voice with his. "When I wear this stole," I said, "I am two thousand years old." The father of the bride looked startled, and then he laughed, and the rest of the wedding rehearsal ran smoothly.

On that particular occasion, my authority was both proclaimed and accepted. I confirmed my authority with a reference the father of the bride could accept; by invoking church tradition, I became older than he was. In turn, he came to recognize the authentic priestly identity of the young woman standing before him. Unfortunately, the rest of my experiences as a young priest have not always run so smoothly. One of the unspoken topics in our church community's life is the issue of Christian authority and age. Because parish communities often equate age with expertise, the unarticulated assumption is that anyone short in years will probably be short on spiritual wisdom as well. My exchange with the anxious father of the bride is emblematic of a critical question our church needs to address: What is the true nature of youth's authority? The well-being of our church depends upon our willingness to move beyond a playful quip about a stole's authority. Instead, we need to recognize that *youth* and *authority* are not mutually exclusive terms; then we must ask ourselves what it would mean to embrace the authority of youth itself, on its own terms, for its own sake.

How *does* the church understand young adults' authority? How do young Episcopalians understand their own spiritual authority? Years of experience as a member and leader of student chaplaincy congregations leaves me with the conviction the church will be transformed as we answer these important questions. In chaplaincies, young adults have created vibrant faith communities that thrive in the midst of our secular age. The authorities they possess and the sources of authority they respect will both challenge and renew our parish churches. In fact, in many ways young adults are already renewing the church, even if we do not yet recognize it fully. The church's task, then, is to become aware of and embrace young adults' authority. The good news is that a gentle spiritual revolution is in the making. If the church wants to survive this revolution, we must turn a critical eye on both our expectations of youth and their expectations of us. If we are going to reflect upon the complex questions of Christian authority and young adults' spiritual authority, we must be willing to live into Christ's triumphant words of transformation: "Behold," says the Christ, "I make all things new" (Rev. 21:5).

CHURCH AND CULTURE'S UNDERSTANDING OF YOUNG ADULTS' AUTHORITY

Like most secular and religious institutions in America, the Episcopal Church tends to picture men and women in their twenties as overgrown adolescents. It has a tendency to emphasize a few select characteristics of youth and to ignore others. For instance, both the church and American culture often extol enthusiasm and high energy as two of the young's greatest characteristics, but they overlook their intelligence and innovation. Television and other media still hold up innocence and naïveté as virtues for young women, and cool disinterest and emotional neutrality are still standards for young men. In addition, young adults' physical prowess—their smooth skin, taut bodies, and white teeth—are idolized to the point of obsession. Our culture's exclusive focus on these traits results in a distorted picture of young adults. We tend to acknowledge only prom queens and football heroes, and their dangerous counterparts, juvenile delinquents. We hammer out caricatures of the complex human beings who make up our current generations of young people.

Unfortunately, the way the church views young adults has been largely determined by the lens of consumer culture. We buy the caricatures our culture's idolization of youth creates. It is both humorous and disappointing to realize that our culture's idolization of young adults blinds us to the people who are actually experiencing their young adulthood. If our young adults can be fit into these superficial ideals, they are dismissed because their lives seem glamorous or easy. Yet if they do not fit, if they are acned, or fat, raw-boned, shy, or slow, they are dismissed because they do not fit the stereotype. Either way, their lives and their opinions are usually disregarded. When young adults also identify themselves as a member of a racial or ethnic minority, the likelihood of their being dismissed becomes even greater. In short, Western culture encourages its members to simplify or glamorize young people's lives, but being young is never simple or easy, and it is rarely glamorous. Young adults' lives are richer, and their true strengths are deeper, more nuanced, and more enduring than this model admits.

SCRIPTURE'S VISION OF YOUNG ADULTS' AUTHORITY

Ironically, scripture's portraits of young people, codified thousands of years ago, provide a more accurate picture of youth than our modern culture's stereotypes. A review of the early lives of three of Christianity's ancestors reveals some of the real challenges young adults face and some of the deep places of power that reside within and around them. The biblical models of David, Mary, and Jesus offer some compelling vignettes of young adults' true authority. By meditating on these stories, we can come to a better understanding of the authority modern young adults are called to claim on campuses and in parishes.

King David was one of the greatest kings Israel has ever known; his reputation as poet, harpist, warrior, ruler, and lover is indisputable. Scripture's stories also retain his capacity for human sin; his greed, his treachery, and his indulgences are recorded in his dealing with Bathsheba, Nathan, and his own children. Yet whether for good or evil, boldness and risk-taking were hallmarks of his kingship, and he was loved for them.

But David's presence at the height of his power stands in contrast to the realities of David's youth. When David was anointed as God's chosen one, neither the prophet sent to fetch him nor the youth's own father, Jesse, considered David to be the best choice for the job (1 Sam. 16). They thought he was too young and inexperienced, and other candidates seemed more qualified. In fact, when Jesse is told to gather his sons he leaves his youngest son David behind, and when the prophet, Samuel, meets Jesse's seven older sons, Eliab, David's oldest brother, impresses him. Samuel decides that Eliab must be God's choice. God has other plans. God rebukes Samuel by reminding him that David contains unexpected but real authority. Says God, "Do not look on his appearance, for the Lord sees not as a human sees; a human looks on the outward appearance, but the Lord looks on the heart" (16:7). Samuel takes this newfound wisdom to Jesse, who finally produces his shepherd boy. David is anointed, but David's elevation to kingship shocks his community because he does not have any of the worldly qualifications required for kingship.

Scripture underscores the point that both God's prophet and David's own father are blind to the authority resting within David. Nevertheless, the authority is there. As David's life unfolds, event after event confirms the unexpected power that stems from David's daring relationship with God. God's audacious choice of David sets David's own audacity in motion. Shepherd becomes court musician, court musician becomes outlaw, outlaw becomes king. The outsider becomes the most intimate of regal insiders, forming strong attachments to both Saul and his son, Jonathan. The one with little promise becomes the boldest, the bravest, the most blessed king of Israel.

David's unexpected authority reaches its first climax when young King David brings the ark of the covenant into Jerusalem. He boldly dances before God and all of Israel as he leads the procession into his city. Scripture asserts that David "danced before God with all his might" (2 Sam. 6:14), an artful phrase that communicates David's total engagement with God. As the story continues, it becomes clear that David is also naked as he dances at the head of the parade. No past liturgical rules, no regal decorum, no standard models of honor or respect mitigate David's proclamation of his intimate connection to God. He shocks the court and his wife, but his people love it.

In his dancing, David does not pierce his navel, as some of the young adults of modern culture do, but he bares his navel, and all the rest of himself for that matter, to reveal his passionate love for God. As David's rise to power suggests, some young adults' exteriors do not hint at the unexpected authority hidden within them. The strong spiritual power that sets the world on its ear can reside in a shy demeanor, or in the heart behind the tattooed chest and the pierced navel. When we least expect it, the young adult next to us may become filled with boldness and vision. The brash authority of the audacious belongs to young King David and to all the young people who find their boldness mirrored in David's story.

———————————◄O►———————————

Mary's story offers a different model of youth's authority. In its quiet way, it is just as powerful as David's story. Mary's annunciation reveals the authority of inexperience; her "yes" to God's angel demonstrates that it is the depth of soul, more than the length of years, that accounts for some young people's authority. Western culture is comfortable affirming the authority that is gained through years of experience, but it has forgotten the powerful and pure authority that resides in the soul regardless of its age. Mary's encounter with

the angel Gabriel teaches our community this lesson. She does not call herself
to the awesome task of becoming Christ's mother, but neither will she shrink
from that call. She is both thoughtful and open to God's possibilities: "How
shall this be?" she asks. As she ponders, the future shape of the entire cosmos
is suspended, and the universe waits upon the answer of a girl.

In a matter of a few moments, she accepts the risk and changes the course
of her life. She does not stall for time to weigh the merits and costs of her
dilemma. She does not refer to experience to make her decision. "Behold," says
Mary, "I am the handmaiden of the Lord; let it be to me according to your
word" (Luke 1:38). Her "yes" is not the naive " yes" of a child, but the soulful
"yes" of a young disciple. She lacks personal experience in the world, but she
does not lack a keen capacity for observing and analyzing the world around
her. Her singing of the Magnificat in Elizabeth's presence a few days later confirms Mary's wisdom about both the harshness and the grace of life. Mary has
an intense love for justice, mercy, and grace, and she perceives the dangers of
this life. In fact, Mary's "yes" to God exposes Mary to some of the world's dangers, shames, and humiliations. If Joseph chose to, he could stone Mary to
death legally because of her "illegitimate" pregnancy, or he could break his
marriage contract with her. Her place in society, even her very life, is thrown
into jeopardy because of her choice. Mary knows this. The story of the annunciation does not glorify naïveté; it glorifies the clear, grounded wisdom that
comes from Mary's different orientation toward the world. Mary's spirit is not
caught up in a tug-of-war between God's call to her and manufactured wants
born out of worldly experience. Her soul is still relatively disengaged from the
compromises, dominations, and oppressions of worldly struggles.

Yet Mary is clear about whose she is. She is "God's handmaiden," and in
knowing her deepest identity Mary finds her answer. Mary gains soulful authority because of her inexperience, and although this authority is often interpreted
as an absence of something, it is not a lack as much as a distinctive orientation
of soul beyond earthly experience. All the young who have taken risks in the
name of justice and love since her time can look back to Mary and recognize
their strength in her answer: "Behold, I am the handmaiden of the Lord."

Like his mother Mary, Jesus himself must come to terms during his youth
with the authority residing within him. Unlike his mother, Jesus is fully divine
as well as fully human, but his divinity does not excuse him from struggling
with his own power as a young man. When the Gospel of Luke describes Jesus'
early life, it confirms that both as a boy of twelve and as a newly minted rabbi,

Jesus had to declare his own readiness for ministry despite the confusion and hostility it caused. First, at the age of twelve, Jesus abandoned his family's Passover caravan in order to remain in the temple and continue studying with the temple's rabbis. Luke 2:41–52 explains that Jesus neither sought permission to stay behind nor worried about his parents' reaction to his three-day absence from them. When his parents found him, scripture says, "They were astonished" (2:48). His mother even scolds him, saying, "Son, why have you treated us so? Behold, your father and I have been looking for you anxiously." Jesus, however, does not understand their anxiety because he understands his own interior truth so well. "Where else would I be?" he asks them in response. His answer is not a flip rudeness; it is a statement about other authorities at work in Jesus. For Jesus, there was simply no other place for him to be, and as a boy he does not yet imagine that his parents would be less astute than he. Jesus acts upon his own internal readiness for learning, whether or not his parents—or anyone else—are prepared for him to do so.

Similarly, as a young rabbi, Jesus proclaims his readiness for ministry in Luke 4:14–30. This time he is wiser about the spiritual limitations of human men and women. As he reads from the Book of Isaiah, Jesus' authority wells up in him like tree sap, and he perceives that his prophetic authority is full blown. "Today, scripture has been fulfilled in your hearing," he tells his neighbors and townsfolk (4:21). When hostility and confusion follow his announcement, Jesus is not surprised. He tells his ruffled neighbors that "no prophet is acceptable in his own country" (4:24). This time he knows that his strong interior truth will not be easy for humans to perceive or accept. Of course, this statement only infuriates his neighbors further, and they resolve to throw him off a cliff; but Jesus' divinity allows him to pass through the crowd and disappear.

In his youth, Jesus models the authority of interior truth. He knows a truth about himself others cannot know, but their inability to perceive his truth does not free him from his responsibility for revealing it. The authority Jesus holds out to us is also a dynamic authority at work in young adults today. They may not be able to articulate their truth fully, but its reference point is deep within their souls and personalities; when it wells up within them, like tree sap, they will proclaim it, whether or not anyone else is prepared to hear it.

———————————◀○▶———————————

The authority of audacity, the authority of inexperience, the authority of interior truth—these are some of the rich sources of power which scripture teaches us that young adults possess. Scripture's images of David, Mary, and Jesus are intended to be prescriptive of young people's authority, as well as descriptive of the particular experiences of the Israelite king, the mother of God, and the Christ. In addition to these three personalities, there are many others, such as Jeremiah and Timothy, who teach us similar lessons. Far from being mascots of white teeth and clear skin, young adults are complex individuals who become complex adults and complex elders. One way to appreciate the authority of the young is to recognize the sources that inspire them. One of our challenges as a church is to confirm and celebrate the wisdom, faith, and authority within them.

YOUNG ADULTS' UNDERSTANDING OF AUTHORITY

In the Pauline epistle to Timothy, the young Christian is encouraged to be stalwart in living out his faith on a daily basis. Timothy's mentor tells him to "let no one despise your youth, but set believers an example in speech, conduct, in love, in faith, in purity" (1 Tim. 4:12). This Pauline wisdom is still a good insight for the college women and men who find themselves free to determine their own schedules and social standards for the first time. Instead of being submerged in the spiritual standards of their families or neighbors, they must choose for themselves their level of curiosity and commitments surrounding God, and their own destinies. However, the young adults who join college chaplaincies can be confident that no one in their church community will "despise their youth," because these spiritual communities are filled with young adults who lead, serve, care for, and learn from one another. Here, young men and women experience themselves as core members of the church, and they are quick to understand the challenges and satisfactions of being "in but not of" the secular community surrounding them. This critical mass of young people invites each person to discover his or her proper place within the community. Not surprisingly, many are awakened to the depths of their own belief when they are surrounded by their peers and encouraged to claim their faith. Chaplaincies take young adults seriously, and young adults respond by taking their own faith seriously.

In fact, chaplaincies have a long tradition of respecting and supporting young adults. Many current church leaders found their first sense of call in an intimate community of their peers. For example, in the past thirty years, twenty-eight priests have been supported by Tulane's Episcopal chaplaincy, and Cornell University has sponsored more than thirty individuals for ordination. Since 1978, Boston University's chaplaincy has supported eight candidates as they journeyed into priesthood, and Harvard University's chaplaincy has produced thirteen priests. By their structure and location, chaplaincies promise to respect the authority of young adults, and young adults respond by forming religious communities that are meaningful to them.

These religious communities provide the larger church with some crucial insights into the future of our parishes and the authority that will prove to be compelling in a postmodern age. An appreciation of these student communities begins with *authority*'s etymology, which brings some useful information into the discussion of youth's authority. *Authority*'s Latin root—*auctoritas*—means "creator," which suggests that to claim or demonstrate one's authority is to reveal oneself to be a creator of something. An authority is one who has the power to influence or to bring about a certain outcome. The young adults in college chaplaincies know how to survive, and even thrive, as Christians in a post-Christian, postmodern setting. Their authority comes from their ability to create solid Christian communities in neutral or hostile territory. These young adults use their own experiences, their intellects, and their emotional intelligence to form dynamic mission communities. When they coauthor their Episcopal communities with God, they co-create religious communities of authenticity, spirituality, and experiential faith. It is these three elements of the Christian tradition that they use to stabilize themselves in a secular world, and it is these elements of our tradition that will stabilize our large network of parishes as our neighborhoods become more secular.

First, students require authenticity from us, and they offer their authentic selves to us in return. They are hungry for honest community—the place where they can search for meaning and purpose in their lives, the place of intimacy and welcome where both the vulnerabilities and the sturdy aspects of their humanity are embraced. Students do not find value in being a part of the institution for the institution's sake; they want to belong to a church only if the others in the community are willing to share real doubts, real griefs, and real successes. In academia's post-Christian, postmodern arena, there is no time for posturing. Keeping the spirit alive means stepping into the promise that God is truly present in all the events of our lives, and then testing out that theory by holding up the concerns and confirmations of a life lived in faith. One of the most popular beginnings of our chapel services at Boston University is the quiet reflection period after the prelude and before the opening sentences. During that pause, the community often takes time to ask ourselves where God has been present in our past week. Then those who wish to share the particular details of their own story do so, and as we listen we support each other in our journeys in faith.

Students are also more interested in the story of each member's faith journey than they are in getting the "right" answer to an issue of faith. They are passionate in their convictions, but they value community over conformity. For instance, the issues surrounding the morality of the death penalty prompted students to discuss not only the moral issues involved, but the stories of the people they knew who held different opinions; their conversation emphasized how people's life experiences affected their opinions. Students also require a community in which time and attention are generously given by the chaplain and the lay members of the church. The model of corporate business, in which schedules are made far in advance, and in which time is jealously guarded, is utterly rejected by these young adults as far as the rhythms of their faith community are concerned. Christian community means showing up for one another in good times and bad. Efficiency and convenience are low priorities; care and commitment are prized.

Second, young adults also prize the mystical and vulnerable reality of spiritual disciplines. In a world where technology produces an overabundance of information, it isn't surprising that these women and men long for the silence, intimacy, and slowness of the spiritual process. Students understand that these disciplines can lead to wisdom and peace—two rare qualities in a nation clamoring with the overstimulation of sound pollution, two-job families, and information superhighways. In his book *Virtual Faith*, which discusses the spirituality of both religious and "nonreligious" Generation Xers, Tom Beaudoin notes, "I have yet to hear an Xer complain of too much silence and darkness during a worship service."[1] My five years as a chaplain confirm his observation. Students long for both. Taizé worship services are enormously popular with students because they are filled with darkness, candles, Christian chanting in many languages, scriptural readings, and silence. These worship services allow members to center themselves in prayer, to open themselves to the meaning of the scripture in their own lives, and to rest in the silence and mystery of God. These students do not reject the intellectual elements of the faith journey, but logic and reason are not the sources of deepest religious meaning for them. They are not anti-intellectual, but they intuitively sense that information about God is not the same thing as knowing God or participating in the spiritual life of God. They want to know God and to be known by God; meditation, spiritual direction, prayer groups, and Taizé worship are the paths they believe will carry them into these holy encounters.

Third, Generation X students are Christian existentialists; concrete experience is a key source of vitality for their spiritual lives. They find meaning and authority in their own lives by placing their whole selves—body, spirit, and mind—into the Christian path. Symbols show up on the bodies of these young adults: crosses are worn both reverently and irreverently, navels and eyebrows may be pierced. Their "secular" music is filled with spiritual references, like Joan Osborn's song "One of Us," which images God "disguised" as a common human being, or Jewel's "Hands," which celebrates prayer and action as faithful responses to the gift of life. Fasting for religious reasons fascinates them. Stations of the cross and the body prayer of the labyrinth spark their imaginations and offer them a sacred journey that engages their whole person. In these actions, they recognize both the vulnerability and the power of witnessing to Christ.

Pilgrimages, both large and small, give these young Christians the opportunity to be consciously open to transforming grace. Working in soup kitchens or homeless shelters, participating in unusual worship services, building houses, cooking Easter dinners—all such experiences engage them because they are both acting out of their faith and living into the new possibilities their faith creates for them. Generation X is committed to acting in the world, but they want to be grounded in a spiritual understanding of the work they do before they act. They want to know where they are standing before they move into new spiritual territory. So they look inward before they turn outward to pastoral actions or actions of social justice. Journeys to Jerusalem or the Taizé community in France provide soul satisfaction for this generation, but pilgrimages to serve inner-city soup kitchens, while less exotic, are no less spiritually satisfying.

Young adults' faith is rigorous, relational, and personal. They announce their belief with their feet, their hands, their music, and their jewelry. Christian Generation Xers live out a ministry of incarnation, inquiry, and action. They respect the authority of candor, the power of spiritual disciplines, the greatness that resides in the mystery of grace, and the transforming dynamic of spiritual pilgrimages.

EMBRACING THE AUTHORITY OF YOUNG ADULTS

Our gospel tells us "not to put new wine in old wineskins" (Mark 2:22) because the wineskins will burst and the new wine will spill onto the floor. But our church often puts young adults into the wineskins of older generations' decorum and conventions in order to acknowledge their authority. When they bring their youthful selves into a parish, they are often subtly required to conform to the worship and community models of their parents' generation, or they are viewed with suspicion. Heather Reed, a senior at Boston University, recently summed up her perspective on this phenomenon. She said, "I have a wonderful experience participating in Episcopal churches, but we young adults always seem to be regarded as the odd participants, rather than core members." Her observation confirms both the spiritual longings of the young and the significant anxieties of older generations. Generation X wants to be a part of a spiritual community, but they don't conform to the expectations of older generations in their social values or religious models.

Older people end up feeling threatened, and younger people feel confused and insignificant. It is time for this standoff to cease. It is not enough for our church to understand young adults' authorities and spiritual commitments; we must embrace them and incorporate them into our parish communities, if we want to flourish in the twenty-first century.

Ironically, the first step toward closing this gap requires the church to acknowledge an even wider gap—the gap between the modern and post-modern social contract. One of the social traditions in this country is the "generation gap," and part of Heather's comment reveals the rite of passage people in their twenties and thirties encounter when they begin to push against the status quo of the generations immediately preceding them. In this country, we expect the young to kick against the values of their elders. However, Heather's comment also touches on an important, but subtle, social revolution taking place in Western culture. Generation X's rite of passage isn't just a generational shift; it's a paradigmatic turn. The whole social contract that determines where meaning and authority are to be found is in the process of being trans-formed. Generation X's transformation into adulthood overlaps with a sig-nificant social watershed; no wonder they are confused and we are anxious.

This new social contract, which has deep roots in the mind-sets of our young adults, has gradually been entering our culture for the past thirty years. Dr. Paul Scott Wilson, professor of homiletics at the Toronto School of Theology, makes note of this fact in his book *The Practice of Preaching*. He explains that "many scholars now point to the difference between the modern social contract, which has been a dominant paradigm since the Enlighten-ment, and the postmodern [social contract], elements which have been co-present but have gradually become dominant ways of describing current social reality."[2] His comprehensive chart further defines this significant water-shed in social values:

The Modern Age	The Postmodern Age
centered	decentered and dispersing
theistic	polytheistic
product- and goal-oriented	process- and service-oriented
vertical idea of authority	horizontal idea of authority
independence/autonomy	interdependence/ relationship
objective/subjective	relative
authority of fact	authorities of interpretation
information	communication

This chart articulates the profound difference between the way individuals over forty and people under forty are inclined to understand where meaning and authority are generated. For instance, the generation that rebuilt American institutions after World War II and the Baby Boomers that attacked the nature of those institutions both believed that power was to be found in a vertical model of authority. They disagreed over the institutions' purposes, but both groups agreed that the institutions themselves were important. However, this modern social contract isn't valid or engaging for young adults. Generation X doesn't define itself either within or against a vertical hierarchy; institutions in and of themselves are not a point of reference. Instead, Generation X finds meaning and significance in a horizontal model of authority. As the postmodern social contract indicates, authority comes from the quality of relationality, from the way a person demonstrates care, love, and justice. Institutions are only as important as the people housed within them. Generation X's orientation toward horizontal models of authority is also one of the reasons that many young adults will assert that they are not "religious," but will enthusiastically claim that they are "spiritual." The word *religious* is associated with institutions that contain vertical ideals of authority, a model that does not engage this generation. But by claiming to be "spiritual," members of Generation X can confirm their connection to God while they also maintain the postmodern preference for a decentered authority that highlights the value of personal truth. Generation X Episcopalians are not less committed than older generations, but they stress different aspects of our faith.

The good news for our church is that the same postmodern social contract that is full blown in the congregations of young adults has already been at work in the life of many of our parish churches. The church is closer to embracing young adults' standards of authority than we might imagine. As Dr. Wilson observed, the postmodern elements redefining where truth and authority are to be found have been co-present with the modern paradigm of truth and authority for some time. The new social contract is lived out most intensely by Generation X because its youth ensures that it is less connected to the social contract of the modern age. But the worshiping styles of many of our parishes have been affected by the power of the postmodern system of authority. This new paradigm of values is reflected in some of the gradual shifts in our church's culture over the past thirty years. Three recent trends within our church underscore the pervasive reality of the postmodern paradigm.

First, the Episcopal Church in the past three decades has become increasingly committed to celebrating "the priesthood of all believers." While we continue to acknowledge the ontological change associated with ordination, we simultaneously hold up the authority given to all believers in their baptism. Since the early sixties, laity have been encouraged to take leadership roles in the liturgy—acting as readers, acolytes, and distributors of the bread and wine—and in the outreach, administration, and pastoral ministry of the church body. Priests and people find their authority together, in a ministry of mutuality. This focus on mutual ministry conforms to one of the most important postmodern principles: the intrinsic value of horizontal authority. We have authority with and through, not over, one another.

Second, our church has been experiencing a renewal in prayer, meditation, and spiritual disciplines. Classes and work groups that experiment with different forms of prayer, including centering prayer, *lectio divina*, Taizé prayer, and silent meditation, have become extremely popular. Their popularity stems from the fact that they feed a deep hunger within the church body. Whether we are lay or ordained, we are experiencing a great longing for an intimate connection to God. We yearn to sense the Spirit around us and within us. These deep longings are fueled by a new postmodern social contract that acknowledges the power of interdependence. We want both to know and to be known by God as distinctive persons, and corporate worship alone does not bring many of us such an intimate sense of relationship to God. The growing popularity of spiritual direction is an especially good example of the authority of intimacy, interpretation, and communication. In spiritual direction, both seeker and mentor practice speaking prayerfully about the daily events of life. Two meet together in the knowledge that God's presence changes the dynamics of the conversation into a prayerful trio; month by month the intimacy among the three develops. The church's growing interest in mysticism and personal spiritual practices underscores that Episcopalians of many ages are shifting into a postmodern system to explore their faith.

Third, it is important to acknowledge the powerful impact healing services have had upon the church's expectations of how we can be present to one another as Christians; this liturgy also claims its power through a postmodern model of authority. The priest or layperson who prays with the congregant has authority because of the love, care, and mercy they exhibit as both priest and person. In addition, the prayer is lifted up to God by one person on behalf of another, honoring the slow process of healing and the slow process of life itself. Whether joys, griefs, or concerns are held up, service is done by one for another. Witnessing to the process of living is done by both the one who prays and the one for whom prayer is offered. Neither knows what the outcome will be, but both trust that God will be in it. In this liturgy, process is valued above result, service is valued over product, interdependency is valued over autonomy, and communication is valued over information. Like spiritual direction, healing services are ancient realities, but they fulfill the expectations postmoderns have about where truth and authority lie. Healing is deeply hoped for, but it is God's work. The human beings engaged in the process are valued for their vulnerability, their intimate conversation, and their personal characters. Each participant is caught up in the mystical process that is powerful because it is decentered, interdependent, and open to interpretation. Such liturgy is a place for communion with God, not for information about God.

———————◄O►———————

The empowerment of the laity, the growth of spiritual disciplines, and the focus on the ministry of healing all point to the positive impact postmodernism has had on the multigenerational church. Our church is already in the process of rediscovering and interpreting the Christian faith to a new world. Young adults are more purely formed by the postmodern contract, so their worship, opinions, doubts, and interests are more purely grounded in the new authorities of postmodernism, but our whole church is on the move. What is required now is acceptance of this quiet revolution. Our parish communities need the faith to consciously engage the transformation taking place and the ability to embrace the spiritual authority young adults offer the church. The facts about our God are not changing, but the manner in which these facts are articulated is changing. The synergy created by a generation's rite of passage and a cultural shift in the social contract is tremendous. But these uncertain times are a faithful expression of the redefining our church has always done to reinterpret the gospel for a new age. We will fail our church only if we choose to ignore the messengers of these changes: our young adults.

If the church wants young adults to be church members, the church community needs to honor the real authority of youth. We must allow ourselves to be awed by the dynamics of their souls, not the wrinkle-free complexions of their faces. We must take their wisdom seriously and risk the discomfort and uncertainty of transition as we welcome them into our congregations. We will be blessed if we open our arms and embrace the changes Generation X presses upon us. We will be blessed if we challenge ourselves to accept young adults' authority as they teach us and lead us. "Behold," says the Christ, "I make all things new" (Rev. 21:5). As we stand on the edge of a new millennium, it is time for the church to say, "Amen."

NOTES

1. Tom Beaudoin, *Virtual Faith: The Irreverent Spiritual Quest of Generation X* (San Francisco: Jossey-Bass, 1998), 168.
2. Paul Scott Wilson, *The Practice of Preaching* (Nashville: Abingdon Press, 1995), 13.

Stole and Stethoscope

Challenges for Formation within the Context of Bivocational Ministry

Daniel Emerson Hall

I am a physician. I am also ordained, and I am embarking on a life-long project to form an integrated bivocational ministry at the interface of faith and medicine. My vision of this particular ministry remains hazy, as if viewed through a glass dimly, but I am confident that this is where God has called me to serve. My medical training will require many more years—even more years than the ordination process! However, even at this early juncture, I recognize that the unique challenges of bivocational ministry add complexity to the already complicated process of forming the identity and ministry of ordained persons. Yet the next generation of clergy have an exciting opportunity to explore new models of ministry as the church adapts to meet the needs of the twenty-first century. Bivocational ministry is not without risk, but I am convinced that it holds rich rewards.

BIVOCATIONAL MINISTRY—A HARD THING TO DEFINE

Perhaps the greatest challenge for formation of bivocational ministry is developing a clear idea of what is being formed. With conventional parochial ministry, the church and its Commissions on Ministry have a fairly clear picture of what ordained ministry might be, and consequently, the goal of formation seems straightforward. But when ordained ministry ventures outside the parochial context, the challenge is acute. In a church polity so completely dominated by parochial models of ministry, it may not even be possible to conceive of ordained ministry outside the parish context.

This difficulty can be appreciated in discussions about ministry. When asked to describe their ministry, Episcopalians often talk about their involvement in the official work of the church. Laypeople teach Sunday school, sing in the choir, make pastoral visits, and serve on committees. Ordained people lead worship, preach, and administer the sacraments. These parochial activities constitute what is most frequently considered to be ministry. While these activities are ministry, this narrow focus on the official work of the church often eclipses the various ministries Episcopalians pursue outside the parochial context in their professional, social, and family lives.

This parochial myopia is common even among bivocational clergy. When asked to describe their ministry, ordained businessmen, lawyers, doctors, professors, and administrators often rely exclusively on "church talk." They define their ministry in terms of preaching, presiding at the Eucharist, or teaching occasional adult education classes. Limiting themselves to a religious vocabulary, they find it difficult to explain how their "secular" work is, in fact, their ministry.

The confusion about bivocational ministry is evident even in the terminology used to identify clergy who also profess another vocation. In addition to "bivocational" clergy, there are three interchangeable terms for dual-career clergy, none of which is adequate. *Nonstipendiary* is problematic because it defines ministry with a negative, stating what it is not rather than making a positive statement about what distinguishes dual-career ministry from traditional ministry. Furthermore, it defines vocation in terms of money, and this is both inaccurate and constraining. The other two terms for dual-career clergy also use financial terms. Although "tent-making" is rooted in the scriptural example of St. Paul, both *tent-making* and *self-supporting* ministries approach the nonparochial vocation as simply the financial means of supporting traditional, parochial ministry. Under these models, the scope and vision of ordained ministry is not influenced or modified by the "secular" vocation.

Of all the options, I prefer the term *bivocational ministry*, because it best accommodates the notion of mutual influence between the ordained and "secular" vocations. However, even this term is inadequate because it implies that there are, in fact, two vocations rather than a single integrated calling. Although bivocational ministers may be involved in the life of a parish, the majority of their time and ministry transpires outside that setting. There they are engaged in a unique form of ministry, exercising their vocation to ordained ministry within the context of their "secular" profession.

Unfortunately, the church does not have adequate language for describing this kind of ministry. Furthermore, with the possible exception of teaching, bi-vocation is sufficiently unusual that there are few examples or role models. While the church does deploy ordained clergy to posts as administrators, educators, and consultants, the ordination processes of most dioceses are designed to discern and test vocations to traditional parochial ministry. Consequently, the existing structures are not completely appropriate for testing or forming bivocational ministry. The church and its committees are not sure how to address the needs of aspirants to bivocational ministry.

For example, my own experience in the ordination process in Connecticut was complicated by general confusion regarding bivocational ministry. Although all the people in the ordination process consistently treated me with respect and integrity, they were often at a loss for what to do with my type of calling. I have never articulated my call to ordination as being lived out exclusively within the context of the parish. Although I will always be attached to a church community, the primary context of my ministry will be in the hospital and the greater medical community. However, the first step in the ordination process in Connecticut is a yearlong period of discernment with a parish committee of laypersons. The scope of my call was beyond their experience, and they had difficulty discerning the proper steps for my formation. In their letter to the bishop, the parish committee wrote, "To a certain extent this particular aspirant falls outside the proper scope of a parish discernment committee. His chief value . . . would seem to be at the diocesan level, an area in which we have no experience to discern."

In some ways, the discernment at the diocesan level was better suited to my particular call to bivocational ministry. However, my ordination was delayed for one year after the completion of my written canonical exams. Several of the explicit reasons for delay focused on concerns that my formation was "incomplete" and on lingering concerns about the theoretical possibility of bivocational ministry. I was instructed to pursue an additional year of supervised ministry in a parochial setting. In hindsight the delay allowed me time to prepare better for ordination. However, it may not always be appropriate to expect full formation before ordination is approved. Christian formation is a lifelong process. Like the riddle of the chicken and the egg, the temporal relation between ordination and formation remains a paradoxical mystery.

Although the committee eventually affirmed my call to ordained ministry with enthusiasm, everyone including myself recognized a fundamental uncertainty about the future shape of my ministry. As one committee member remarked, the committee was not certain where my ministry would take me, but they were willing to open the door and to let me fly freely into the wind.

A MODEL FROM MISSIONS

The previous discussion exposes some of the confusion about the nature of bivocational ministry. However, it does not provide an interpretive framework for understanding such ministry as an integrated whole, greater than the sum of its two parts. If the formation of persons for bivocational ministry is to proceed with integrity, it must be rooted in solid theology. Before addressing distinctly sacramental aspects of bivocational ministry, it is important first to understand how it might fit into the wider ministry of the church as the church lives into its baptismal covenant. While there are several possible approaches, the most helpful model might be drawn from a theology of mission.

When I share my plans to be both a physician and a priest, most people assume that I intend to pursue some form of missionary work. Drawing from the model of Albert Schweitzer, they assume that the best place to pursue medicine as ministry is within the context of mission to a developing country. Although this is one possible context for bivocational ministry, my own experience as a missionary teacher in Zimbabwe convinced me that my gifts are better suited to the cultural context of the United States. However, this does not mean that I have abandoned the call to mission.

Mission is fundamentally a cross-cultural experience. The missionary travels to a part of the world where the gospel has not been preached. Entering that world, the missionary learns a new language, cuisine, custom, and culture. By learning to see the world through new eyes, the missionary learns to love in new ways, seeing beyond surface differences to recognize the image of God in the faces of previously unknown people. If the communication is genuine, the missionary and his or her new community will grow together as they discover the movement of the Holy Spirit in their midst.

I view my bivocational ministry as a form of mission. Unlike traditional mission, the goal is not the conversion of souls or the planting of churches. The goal of mission is not the spread of "religion," but the spread of the good news of Christ Jesus. As a bivocational physician priest, I am a witness to Christ in a new and foreign context. Through my medical training, I have learned a new language, custom, and culture. I have become "one of the natives." Although the customs are at times disturbing, and although not all parts of medicine are lovable, I am growing to love and respect physicians and health care professionals for their dedication to the difficult and often unrewarding job of caring for the sick.

Although I approach medicine as a form of Christian mission, medicine is a "secular" profession, and it is appropriate that it remain so. However, medicine is engaged in a moral enterprise that is part of God's created order. As such I believe that the goals of medicine will be best fulfilled when the care of patients is conducted according to the love of Christ crucified. This does not require that all hospitals conduct their business "in the name of Jesus." This sectarian approach is too narrow. Instead, I am suggesting that even in a "secular" context, the best type of medical care would order its relations with patients and colleagues according to the love and respect revealed in the Triune God.

This perfect ordering of relations within medicine will not be fulfilled until the completion of creation at Christ's second coming. However, as a missionary to the community of medicine, my task is to reveal (perhaps in "secular" terms) the ways in which medicine might better order its corporate life according to the divine economy. Part of my work as a bivocational missionary to the hospital is to offer a Christian witness as the medical profession continues to work toward achieving its goal of caring for the sick.

For example, there has been a recent explosion of interest in the general public concerning alternative and complementary health care. This interest is indicative of a deep hunger not being fed by the current practice of Western medicine. The precise nature of this hunger is unclear, but the appeal of alternative health care systems seems to be their philosophical frameworks, through which a patient can make sense of what it means to be sick. I propose that the attraction of alternative health care is found less in its efficacy than in its facility with finding meaning in illness.

On the other hand, in its success and zeal for effectively treating disease, Western medicine has largely abdicated its role as the interpreter of illness in favor of the promise of scientific efficacy. Both patients and physicians have come to believe that sickness and death would be preventable if only we knew enough science. As a result, the reality of sickness is all the more shocking when it breaks into our otherwise tidy lives. When that happens, patients and their families often turn to their physicians for guidance in making sense of suffering. In the current era of increasingly complex medical technology, it is more important than ever that physicians cultivate their skills at helping patients interpret their illness in meaningful ways. Part of my ministry will be to help physicians refine their skills at addressing the issues of meaning and value, connecting each patient to the social, philosophical, and spiritual resources that help break the isolation of sickness and suffering.

This goal is not explicitly Christian. However, the project is religious insofar as the discipline of addressing questions of meaning and value is fundamentally religious. If I can encourage others to ask the right types of questions, I have confidence that their own curiosity will eventually lead them to the Triune God revealed to us in the person of the incarnate Christ. Through my witness, I may help medicine move a small step closer to its intended purpose, which is the enjoyment of God above all else through the care of the sick and suffering. This is my call to mission.

HEALING THE DIVISION BETWEEN "SACRED" AND "SECULAR"

The skeptic might challenge my assertion that medicine has an "intended purpose." However, in that challenge is found the key to understanding my approach to bivocational ministry. The challenge is predicated on the common assumption that our world is divided into two separate and independent realms called the "sacred" and the "secular." I believe that this is a false dichotomy, and the reader will notice that each reference to the "secular" is enclosed by quotation marks because I consider it an artificial construct. Although the church, particularly in the West, has often acquiesced to this false dichotomy, I do not believe it is consistent with the Christian witness.

God created all things, sun and stars, land and sea, birds and beasts—and all were good. God also created people, but human beings are unique in that they are created in God's image. Our unique vocation is to enjoy God above all else, or as the Eastern Orthodox would say, to be in communion with God. However, this communion is not limited to a disembodied, "spiritual" communion. Rather, humans are to enjoy God with all that they are: body, mind, and spirit. To that end, God prepares all of creation for human stewardship, giving people "dominion over it" so that through stewardship we might participate in the communion of God. God is the source of all life, and as we eat our food, cultivate our fields, and order our societies, we participate in that life and thereby commune with God.

However, we do not always see the world in this way. We often approach creation as an end in itself rather than as an instrument of communion. To the extent to which we view it this way we are idolatrous. Food becomes the necessary source of life rather than a means of communion. Work becomes the agency by which we secure and maintain our existence rather than a means of participating in God's ordering of life. This is the sin of the forbidden fruit. The fruit of the "tree of the knowledge of good and evil" is the one part of creation not given to humankind, yet Adam and Eve eat it anyway. Rather than eating as an act of communion with God, they eat the fruit for its own sake to gain knowledge of good and evil—in order to become like gods—and the result is broken communion with God. The "apple" is the first instance of the false dichotomy between "sacred" and "secular," whereby humans choose to separate God from God's creation, confining God to the "sacred" and reserving the "secular" for themselves.

God, however, is not content to leave humanity in its isolation, and through Christ, God restores for us the possibility of full communion. From the "secular" perspective, the chain of life flows up the food chain from the base of the food pyramid to its pinnacle, which is humanity. But this perspective fundamentally distorts the true source of life, which flows from God down the food chain to all that lives and moves on the face of the earth. The mystery of the Eucharist reveals the true source of life as Christ, who gives himself to us in the form of bread and wine. The top of the "food pyramid" becomes the bottom so that humans might know the true ordering of life.

Unfortunately, the structure of contemporary American culture perpet-
uates the false dichotomy between "sacred" and "secular," driving an artificial
wedge between public and private lives. The working world is completely separate from the worshiping world. Religion is relegated to the realm of personal
experience, while work is part of the public forum. To some extent, the church
has capitulated to these assumptions insofar as it has focused primarily on the
worship life of the community. Given the cultural context that separates work
and worship, it is less surprising that despite attempts to "empower the laity,"
the church continues to struggle with the Sunday-Monday connection.

But Christ did not redeem only our worship life. God creates, redeems,
and sanctifies all aspects of our life. In the late-twentieth-century context, the
church may be uniquely poised to witness to a more integrated view of human
life in which our work becomes our worship, "so that we might present ourselves as a living sacrifice, holy and acceptable to God, which is our spiritual
worship" (Rom. 12:1). Indeed, I would argue that this is the fundamental mission of the church: In a world as disintegrated and isolated as ours, the church
is called to reveal the innate connectedness of all aspects of human life to each
other and to God in Christ Jesus.

The goal of mission is not, therefore, merely the planting of churches or the
creation of new parochial communities. Such traditional mission simply maintains the parochial structures of the church, and this in turn may reinforce the
false dichotomy between "secular" and "sacred." Rather, the goal of mission is to
reveal to the world that all aspects of human life, including our public and working lives, are created as means for communion. Such communion is accomplished
by grace through personal devotion, corporate worship, the proper ordering of
our working lives, and a joyful sense of play to inspire our leisure time.

All baptized Christians are called by the Great Commission to participate in
this mission. The church sends its people into the world to do their work as witnesses to Christ. Although the church sends people out from a community of worship into their various workplaces, the church does not cease to be the church. The
church is just as much a church in the office building as it is in the sanctuary.

In some sense, all baptized Christians are bivocational ministers. Rather
than traveling to a geographical location where the gospel has not been
preached, they travel to an equally foreign place within the existing community where the gospel is not always heard—their place of work. There they
can witness to a more integrated approach to life where even the working
world is approached as a form of communion with God. I am not proposing the creation of chapel services within corporate office buildings. Rather,
I am suggesting a more fundamental shift in perspective in which the substance of our "secular" work is approached as worship.

Finally, before addressing the issue of ordination, one additional aspect of mission deserves attention: evangelism. Unlike traditional mission, this expanded notion of mission is not limited to evangelizing particular people, although this may be appropriate. Instead, part of the church's mission to the hospital might be seen as an attempt to evangelize the system. Walter Wink proposes an interesting model for understanding the systems that order our common lives.[1] He observes that systems, like the market economy, race relations, or even church politics, have a life of their own in which the system is larger than the sum of the individual people of whom it is made. Identifying these systems as the "powers and principalities" mentioned in scripture, Wink proposes that they were created by God to govern and order our common life, but that like the rest of creation, they are fallen and in need of redemption. God, however, intends these powers and principalities as instruments for communion.

Medicine is one such system. Although many might disagree, medicine is not a business. It is not about money, power, influence, or cost containment. Instead, it is about the fundamentally moral enterprise of caring for sick people. As such, medicine is an essential part of the church's ministry. More than just ordering the worship lives of its people, the church fulfills its role as Christ's body on earth by caring for the sick and suffering. The church can achieve this only through cooperation with the "power and principality" of the medical system. To the extent that the medical system is not properly focused on its mission, it remains in need of evangelism and conversion.

WHY BE ORDAINED?

Given this expanded notion of mission, it would seem that the full potential of ordained ministry is limited if constrained to the parochial setting. The life of the church would be enriched if it sent ordained ministers into various communities of work to represent the church, by leading, empowering, and equipping lay people in their working ministry. However, even if the ministry of a bivocational physician priest is accepted as a form of mission to the "mission field" of medicine, it is not obvious why the missionary should be ordained. It is not clear what an ordained physician priest offers by virtue of his or her bi-vocation that cannot be offered by either a mono-vocational physician or a mono-vocational priest. Why then, should some physicians be ordained? This is what people often asked during my ordination process.

The question is particularly acute in the context of "the priesthood of all believers" articulated in the 1979 *Book of Common Prayer*. It might seem that a certain version of lay ministry is exactly the sort of ministry I propose within the working community of medicine. To a certain extent, this is true. The 1979 prayer book made an appropriate shift away from clericalism by insisting that the clergy are not a superior class of Christians. All Christians are baptized into the priesthood of all believers. However, I fear that the current interpretation of the "priesthood of all believers" may shackle the church to a limited understanding of ordained ministry. In struggling to affirm the "priesthood" of the laity, we may impoverish our understanding of ordination, reducing it to the functional role of presiding over the sacraments.

Although this functional theology of ordination is in ascendancy, it fails to account for the multiple layers of meaning in ordination. The vocation of priesthood is not limited to presiding over the sacraments and making them "valid." Rather, much of the ordained vocation grows from the priest's unique role as someone set apart from the community whose very identity is thereby transformed into a sacrament. This approach to ordination is easily distorted to perpetuate patterns of clericalism. As a result, aspirants and Commissions on Ministry are frequently reluctant to speak openly about the ontological aspects of understanding and forming ordained ministry. However, it is essential to recognize some sense of the transformed identity of ordained persons.

For example, although not the arbiter of theological truth, the works of religious anthropologists such as Eliade, Turner, and Lévi-Strauss have described persuasively how, in almost every society, ordination changes the ontological identity of the ordained person within the life of the community. Ordinands are set apart, and much of their role beyond the administration of sacraments stems from their changed identity. In fact, if viewed through the eyes of an anthropologist, it might be argued that much of the focus on "formation" in the ordination process is directed toward cultivating an awareness and understanding of this new identity.

When approached through such a robust sense of the ontological identity of ordination, the unique witness of bivocational clergy is better appreciated. For example, in the case of bivocational physicians, there is something powerful and persuasive about the witness of someone who is both physician and priest. At conferences addressing the interface of faith and medicine, various people come together to discuss the common subject. Each person speaks from his or her own perspective as physician, nurse practitioner, chaplain, or patient. In some sense, each operates outside the "interface" that the conference seeks to address. However, as an ordained physician, I live at the intersection between faith and medicine. Consequently, by virtue of who I am and where I live my life, my perspective on issues of faith and medicine carries intrinsic weight. If I were not both an ordained clergyman and a practicing physician, my identity and my perspective would not be the same.

A SACRAMENTAL APPROACH

The preceding example of the power of bivocational ministry is only empirical, and although it may inspire new insight, it does not establish normative theology for the church. Before the practice of bivocational ministry is widely adopted, it must be rooted in a solid theological framework. To that end, attention must be directed to sacramental theology. As traditionally understood, sacraments are part of the worship life of the church, and the primary examples are baptism and Eucharist. However, ordination is itself a sacrament, and the ordained clergy are appointed to preside over the other sacraments of the church. Because of this special, sacramental role, clergy can be perceived as mediators between the natural and supernatural realms. As previously discussed, this error of clericalism is rooted in the false dichotomy between "sacred" and "secular." If in fact there is no division between our "sacred" and "secular" lives, the roles of sacraments and of the ordained clergy who administer them become less clear. As the church community expands beyond the parochial setting it is not clear how the church ministers sacramentally in the context of the community of work.

Part of the confusion grows from the fact that, in the West, the church is constrained by Western categories of sacramental theology that tend to focus on how sacraments "work" and on what makes them "valid," rather than describing how they become a transforming act. Through the transforming act of a sacrament we encounter the world as the kingdom of God redeemed and restored by Christ, but somehow, at the same time, as a world groaning for the completion of that redemption and restoration.

Properly understood, sacramental ministry ought not to be limited to the context of parochial worship. Rather, as a transforming event that reveals the integrated nature of all creation, the sacramental ministry of the church ought to be as vibrant within "secular" communities of work as it is in the "sacred" communities of worship. Consequently, the sacramental ministry of bivocational clergy might be expressed in the following terms.

Christians believe that through the incarnation, God entered completely into the human experience. From this central belief follows the conviction that God is equally present in the intensive care unit and in the church sanctuary. Unfortunately, like most spiritual truths, this is not always obvious. The systems that govern our common life are not always aligned with God's order, and there often appears to be an insurmountable barrier between "sacred" and "secular," faith and science, chaplain and physician.

However, God ordains sacraments as "outward and visible signs of inward and spiritual grace." As such, the life of an ordained physician might be considered a sacrament. It is the outward and visible sign—the living conviction—that the apparent gulf between faith and medicine is, in fact, an illusion. The sacramental identity of the ordained physician becomes a transformation, a passage, perhaps even an icon through which the integrated nature of all creation is manifest. This iconic role of the clergy may persist even outside the worshiping assembly. Through the "sacramental" life of an ordained physician, Christ asserts the truth that through his incarnation he has drawn all things to himself in perfect unity, and, through him, into unity with the Triune Godhead. Through Christ, the chasm is filled, the system is redeemed, and the division between faith and medicine is healed.

For example, the eucharistic elements are a tangible and paradoxical mystery that force Christians and non-Christians alike to ask the question of how the apparently ordinary bread and wine can be the body and blood of Christ. The contemplation of this mystery leads those who have eyes to see toward the transcendent reality of God. In a similar way, the witness and identity of a physician priest is a tangible and paradoxical mystery. The presence of that sacramental life challenges the assumption that faith and medicine are incompatible.

Furthermore, the eucharistic sacrament provides nourishment and reassurance to Christians as they struggle to view the world through the eyes of faith and to order their lives according to God's economy. Given that Christians spend most of their lives in the working world, might not the presence of a physician priest offer similar reassurance as people struggle to approach their working lives as spiritual worship? As lay health care workers toil to realize the unity between faith and medicine intended by God's economy, the sacramental presence of a physician priest in their midst might offer reassurance of the unity for which they strive.

With fewer and fewer people attending churches today, bivocational clergy have a unique opportunity. Through their sacramental presence the church can send itself into the world, sanctifying the work of its people and providing ministers to help guide and equip their labors in the working community. Through bivocational ministry the church can take seriously the call for evangelism and adapt its mission to the contemporary context.

This sacramental approach to bivocational ministry is powerful, but it may not yet find widespread acceptance because it stretches the traditional understanding of sacrament beyond the narrowly defined context of parochial life. However, I do believe it is orthodox. In fact, it may even be Orthodox—my thought has been influenced by Orthodox theology, particularly the work of Alexander Schmemann.[2] However, such Orthodox sacramental theology may continue to taste strange on the Western palate that reinforces the dichotomies of "sacred" and "secular," relegating sacraments to a parochial ghetto.

In the specific context of medicine in which physicians are already prone to a "god complex," it is important to qualify this sacramental theology by noting that this approach runs the risk of confusing the sign with the truth signified by that sign. That is to say, while the sacramental life of an ordained physician is a powerful sign of Christ (perhaps even an icon), the ordained physician makes no claim actually to be Christ. Ordained physicians can never fully substantiate that which their sacramental lives represent. Even using such language as "substantiation" begins to apply Western categories of "validity," which have confused and constrained the full richness of sacramental theology.

Finally, the risk of this sacramental approach is that bivocational clergy will become mavericks, cut off from the life of the church, working in some uncharted community by witnessing to Christ through the "sacrament of their lives." However, as the preceding discussion implies, any adequate theology of sacrament defines it within the life of the church. It makes no sense to speak of a sacramental ministry that is "maverick" and cut off from the greater life of the church. Sacraments do not exist in a vacuum. They are gifts of God to the church, and it is the church that acts as the steward of sacraments, ordaining and administering their distribution by God's will. Sacraments flow from God through the church and out into the wider community and the world. Although the sacrament of a particular life is personal, it does not fall under the stewardship of that person alone, isolated from the community of faith. Rather, the church is the steward of that bivocational sacrament, and it is the church that is commissioned by God to ordain and administer that sacramental ministry.

As discussed earlier, the church is not confined to the sanctuary. The church extends beyond the sanctuary to the mission field, the monastic cloister, the desert hermitage, the wheat fields, the courtroom, and the assembly line. Bivocational ministers interested in extending the sacramental presence of the church to these working communities must remain connected with the church, its worship, and structure. However, the church may need to respond by expanding its own notion of the scope of sacramental ministry. In this way, the work of a bivocational physician priest remains firmly rooted in the church community as a missionary to the wider community of medicine, expanding the church's presence and exercising a sacramental ministry that reveals and heals the community as it seeks better ways to discharge its work of caring for the sick and suffering.

PRACTICAL CHALLENGES FOR FORMATION

This essay started with the assertion that the greatest challenge for formation of bivocational ministry is developing some clear sense of what is being formed. Now that I have outlined a preliminary sketch of what bivocational ministry might look like, it is possible to return to the question of formation.

To a large degree, formation of a sacramental identity is a communal endeavor. What starts in the tight-knit community of seminary continues as clergy move into their first positions and start to live into their identity as ordained ministers of the church. For bivocational ministers this process can be problematic, because they rarely have a community of similar people to help them shape and form their identity. In an attempt to find such a community, I conducted a study of eighty-three physician clergy in the Episcopal Church. The variety of career paths represented in the study group was practically unlimited, and each person navigated uncharted waters in his or her career development. As a result, most developed their ministry in isolation from one another with little conversation or support from other physician clergy or from other bivocational clergy. Such isolation magnifies the challenge of developing adequate language and theology for describing bivocational ministry, and as a result, there was little consensus among the physician clergy about the nature and practice of bivocational ministry. Furthermore, isolated from one another, these physician clergy did not have a community to hold one another accountable for approaching medical practice in ways intentionally rooted in their identity as ordained clergy. This might explain why the surveyed physician clergy were not appreciably different from their "secular" colleagues.

Even traditional clergy find isolation to be a problem. As discussed previously, by virtue of their ordination, clergy are separated from ordinary society. They consistently struggle to maintain networks of support with other clergy with whom they can form and shape their ministries and identities. However, because there are so few bivocational clergy, the problem of isolation is significantly more acute for this group. Furthermore, the demanding schedule of bivocational ministry often works against good intentions to dialogue with other clergy.

I suspect that the successful formation of bivocational ministry depends on a vibrant community of bivocational ministers with whom each might test and shape his or her identity. To that end, physician clergy might profit from more extensive dialogue with one another as well as with other bivocational clergy. Together they might develop a better and more adequate language for describing their work. Furthermore, they might serve as a community of accountability in which their identities will take on distinctive qualities that differentiate them from both "secular" professionals and parochial clergy.[3]

The conversation might be further enriched if extended to include the wider church. The church will hold bivocational ministers accountable to the historic sacrament of ordination, reigning in mavericks and refining the germinal attempts to understand this unique ministry. At the same time, bivocational ministers might help the church break out of the shackles of seeing itself and the community through the exclusive perspective of worship. Together they might develop a new sense of evangelism that moves beyond the sanctuary pew to meet people in their places of work. Together they might reclaim as sanctified the working lives of all Christian people in an attempt to restore a sense of Christ's meaning and unity to our increasingly fragmented lives.

The task of articulating a sacramental theology of bivocational ministry is daunting. Even a world-class theologian would find it challenging to resolve all the problems. This essay is not offered as the solution, but it is my hope that it helps frame some of the issues. If I am on the right track, and if the Episcopal Church wants seriously to pursue the full potential of bivocational ministry, there are several positive actions that might help. The church might facilitate the formation of such bivocational ministry by taking stock of its assumptions about ordained ministry. It might actively raise up and encourage bivocational ministers by searching out those persons who share some of the vision to become a sacramental presence within various working communities. In the ordination process, the church might assist the formation of bivocational clergy by expanding expectations beyond the formation of parochial clergy only. Bishops, Commissions on Ministry, and seminaries could all become more familiar with nonparochial forms of ordained ministry, remaining open to the ways God may be calling leaders to new forms of ministry. In this way, those called to nonparochial ministry might be able to articulate with integrity their own calling rather than being forced to conform their vision to a parish model for the sake of surviving the ordination process. Most of all, the church could assist the formation of bivocational clergy by connecting them with other bivocational ministers in order to foster the kind of community in which formation is best achieved.

NOTES

1. Walter Wink, *Engaging the Powers: Discernment and Resistance in a World of Domination* (Philadelphia: Fortress Press, 1992).
2. Alexander Schmemann, *For the Life of the World: Sacraments and Orthodoxy* (Crestwood, N.Y.: St. Vladimir's Seminary Press, 1963).
3. A complete report of my study of ordained physicians as well as an attempt to catalyze a community of physician clergy with an E-mail listserve can be found at www.members.tripod.com/~physicianclergy.

SECTION THREE

THE CHANGING FACES OF ORDAINED MINISTRY

ISO PEER GROUP

Episcopal Culture through an Xer Lens

Beth Maynard

Like most seminarians, I had to take a course in pastoral ministry. In fact, I took two, one at an Episcopal seminary and one at a non-Episcopal seminary. In the latter class, the professor assigned us a book that covered how "we" could most effectively minister to Baby Boomers. I remember making careful notes with absolutely no sense of irony. Here I was, younger at age thirty than the "young adults" in the text, yet automatically viewing its advice from the point of view of an establishment that would have to adapt in order to reach a new generation—in this case, Baby Boomers. It honestly never dawned on me that I was not part of that "we."

Looking back, I now see that this attitude had been instilled in me through a decade of involvement in the Episcopal Church. After becoming a Christian at age seventeen, I discovered that being active in a parish required surrounding myself with persons at least fifteen to twenty years older than I was. The age gap didn't bother me, however, because I was happily mesmerized by all the things I had to learn to belong in this alien, churched world.

So they socialized me. A lot of it was good: where to find important things in the Bible. How to feel when the church is clothed in purple. What to say in response to "The Lord be with you." But along with that spiritual formation came other unspoken requirements. I had to learn to see the rules and protocols of the institutional church as important. I had to be willing to keep my native sense of irony to one side.[1] I had to know that the kind of music I listened to, the way I preferred to dress, the media that interested me, and so on were not part of "our" culture. While I could enjoy these things outside the church, inside I had to adapt, because "we" didn't do things that way.

Frankly, I wanted God so much I was willing to put up with it. Anything that seemed to go along with the privilege of getting to receive Christ in the Eucharist, I swallowed wholesale. It was more important to me to have an Episcopal peer group than a peer group my own age.

Over a decade, identifying with that group and living in that climate had a powerful shaping influence. As I moved into lay leadership in the church in my early twenties, the shaping went further. I got good at talking to fifty-year-olds and proposing ideas that would fit in their structures. I learned how "we" usually explained the things "we" care about, without ever actually asking whether I cared about them myself or not. I practiced locating myself on the maps my elders had drawn. I often vaguely wished this litmus-test mapping wasn't part of the game, but I couldn't imagine other options.

Six years after graduating from college, I finally gave in to a persistent call to ordination. I was twenty-eight years old. The shaping continued; and again, much of it was good. I read Richard Hooker and was moved to tears by his descriptions of the Eucharist. I prayed the Office daily and started dancing to the rhythms of the liturgical year. Wise presbyters mentored me and told me stories of their ministries.

But along with that formation came more subtle information about how "we" were to see things. I dutifully followed and honored the byzantine channels of the 1990s ordination process, so clearly geared to people at midlife. For instance, I tried to feel appreciative when one priest I approached to talk about ministry responded by giving me an article on clerical dysfunction, listing statistics of drug abuse and divorce. I tried to understand the perspective of interviewers who seemed more concerned about making sure I invoked Baby-Boomer buzzwords like "wounded healer" and "vulnerability" than about my love for Christ and the church. I tried to take cues from the much more numerous midlife seminarians who kept dropping remarks about postulants who were too young to know anything because, after all, they had never suffered.

The power of all that socialization can perhaps be measured by the fact that I somehow kept myself from getting especially angry about most of it. Maybe I should have gotten angry, but I honestly assumed all those people must be right. This was how "we" did things; as a minority, I should be grateful, and learn my place.

It was about a year after ordination that God began to shake loose the shackles of my denial. Safely through what everyone called The Process, I read a book on Generation X—again, to learn how "we" should minister to them—and something inside me whispered, "Hey, wait a minute. What were those birth dates again?"

Comparing the generational characteristics I was studying with my limited experience of the few clergy who fit the GenX demographic, I found that these characteristics made sense. I cautiously began to form a working hypothesis: first, that what I had been in the habit of thinking of as my own idiosyncratic perspectives on the church might be generationally influenced; and second, that Episcopalians my age might share some of them. (Of course, as I joked to colleagues, how reliable can a hypothesis be with a sample size of seven?)

It was attending the "Gathering the NeXt Generation" conference, which not only convinced me that we did share distinctive perspectives, but which even provided a three-day immersion in them. I had never imagined anything like it. There was another "we" out there within the Episcopal Church, and it thought, laughed, worshiped, and critiqued strangely like me. Until discovering my generational peer group, I had accepted the amalgam of Episcopal culture as simply the way "we" did things. But at GTNG, that amalgam broke apart. Now it seemed that at least some—how much?—of what I had absorbed over those years of shaping had been values and customs of the "silent" and GI generations in the pews and of the Baby Boomers who had made it into the ranks of our clergy and lay leadership. The Episcopal Church that I loved turned out to be wrapped in generational *adiaphora*.[2]

I went to GTNG to test a hypothesis, but the hypothesis ended up testing me. Now that it was clear that there were distinctive perspectives, I began to wonder whether knowing this fact made me responsible in some way. If this new "we" had our own way of being in the church, what was it and how could we put it into action? If it was possible to be an Episcopal leader while remaining culturally true to my own generation, didn't I need to find out how to do that? Wasn't that kind of leadership precisely what our graying and isolated denomination needed? And finally, might we Xers be able to offer unique service to the church's mission to "restore all people to unity with God and each other in Christ"?[3]

I am still far from having answers to those questions, but I do have clues that point toward answers. Those clues often come when I attend to, rather than repress, the feelings of discontinuity that arise as I go about being a priest in this church. I have begun to pay more attention to how I feel at diocesan events, in clergy gatherings, while reading the Episcopal press, and I often ask myself deliberately what my reaction would be if I were not in an official Episcopal setting, but at home or with secular friends.

It turns out that there are plenty of discontinuities, and they come in two basic flavors. First, I encounter habits and assumptions in the church that I formerly assumed were simply facts of life in the Episcopal context, but now seem clearly to me to be optional expressions of another generation's style and concerns. Second, I notice the conspicuous absence in the church of things that are an ordinary part of life everywhere else.

The second category can be described more quickly than the first. Take music, for example. I am not a big radio or MTV fan, but I know what music people listen to; I know what the score of a contemporary film or TV commercial sounds like. I have rarely heard anything similar in an Episcopal setting. The closest has been an amplified combo playing praise songs from the early 1970s. Don't get me wrong: it wouldn't be Advent 4 without "Lo he comes with clouds descending" sung to Helmsley; I relish hearing a choir perform Parry and Byrd. But why does life inside the church always have to have a completely different soundtrack from life outside the church?

Take the issue of cultural allusion. Here's an event that happens with some frequency: I will find a snippet of pop culture that seems telling or comical, and as a conscientious, incarnationally oriented Anglican preacher, I will imagine using it in a sermon. But just as I get that quotation from Homer Simpson, Monty Python, or the Blues Brothers honed, I hear the voice of the internal censor I have had to develop: we don't allow those sections of life, thanks. First, hardly anyone in the congregation will understand the reference, and second, those who do are likely to think that it doesn't belong in church.

The same kind of thing goes on in other church settings. A youth-group activity from a respected curriculum suggests critiquing a video by Madonna. The suggestion is vetoed by a lay leader as "inappropriate for church," even though we are all aware that many parishioners (and not just teenagers) enjoy such things every day. I get a mailing from an Episcopal group urging us all to oppose a TV program as antireligious and corrosive to Christian values; the problem is, I love the show. A bright, capable young woman shows up with a piercing, and the same people who nominated her for vestry begin whispering to each other, "She isn't going to wear that, is she?"

I have heard similar anecdotes from 1960s clergy who tried to bring their counterculture experience into the church of that era, but the similarity may ultimately break down. Thirty years ago, a stable, majority institution was being challenged by marginal voices; today it is the institution that is on the margins, isolating itself from the masses who live and breathe popular culture. Thanks to the escalation of social change, mainline churches can no longer claim merely to be resisting trendy youth fads or radical counterculture; they have come to stand, confused and well-meaning, in a thoroughgoing cultural isolation.

So let's be a little more impressionistic here. Take advertising. I think it's just part of life; the silent/GI-generation parishioners I talk to think it is secular and grasping, and that for a church to employ advertising would compromise our integrity. Take slogans. Take images. Take typefaces, for crying out loud. I'd rather play with fonts like Onyx or Juice ITC, while the people who want a new sign for the parish hope it can be commissioned in Olde English Script. Even the most current Episcopal promotional materials nearly always look dated to me. On the other hand, I respond immediately and viscerally to congregational materials designed for and by Xers who are unafraid of the language of image and allusion fluently spoken throughout our society.[4]

Some laity still find it fanciful that their parish has a Web page, and some clergy proudly boast that they don't know how to use the Internet and never plan to learn. (If you want to know how this sounds to me, substitute "telephone" in the sentence. Substitute "car." Substitute "electric light.")

The world we live in at the turn of the millennium, like all creation, is fallen and fallible. Yet it is no less capable of bearing the infinite than any other world. The church, however, is increasingly alienated from our world, and the gap seems to be widening. As Kevin Graham Ford writes, "A profound generational and cultural shift has already taken place."[5] Whether consciously or not, by failing to notice this shift and to engage those of us on the other side of it, the institutional church is closing its doors to new examples of incarnation and becoming deaf to the sighs of the Spirit, who calls out too deeply for words.

Thus, the first major type of discontinuity are those aspects of culture that remain conspicuously absent in church. And then there is the other type, harder to sort out: practices taken for granted in the Episcopal context that now seem to me as expressions of a former era's culture. At best, these practices are optional; at worst, they are hurting the church's cause. Five instances of this type of discontinuity have become especially jarring to me, and I wish I could write about them in hypertext, because they are all messily interlinked. However, given the limitations of hard copy, they will have to line up neatly one after another: the reduction of faith into social causes; the attempt to be contemporary by secularizing; the zest for infighting and polarization; the channeling of energy into governance; and—the notion that undergirds them all—the persistent loyalty to the paradigm of Christendom.

The reduction of faith into social causes is a key area of discontinuity. I am beginning to notice how misguided it feels when I watch the Episcopal Church promoting Christianity and Jesus as a means to something else, whether it be self-actualization, family stability, diversity, feminism, or peace and justice. I learned in seminary, from the innumerable times I was assigned and reassigned H. Richard Niebuhr's *Christ and Culture*, that we were supposed to behave this way. We Anglicans, with F. D. Maurice leading the way, were the heroes, the cool Christ-transforming-culture group who got a favored spot at the end of the book, spared all critiques and poised to bring in the kingdom.[6]

And so Episcopalians characteristically try to improve things on various fronts. Many of the political and personal goals that members of our denomination identify as the expression of their Christian faith are important, and these goals provide a crucial fleshing-out of the gospel message for people who have already accepted it. A Christianity devoid of concern for justice would be hollow. But it is obvious to Xers that many non-Christians are also working toward bettering themselves and the world; their stories about what motivates them, which may cite their own faith or no faith at all, seem equally plausible. If we want opportunities to serve a cause or to grow as persons, we Xers are more likely to sidestep the question of underlying rationales and just do the work. Trying to identify that work with Christianity strikes many of us as nonsensical.[7] When we look to a religion, we are looking for something more.

It's easy to find a recovery support group, a domestic-violence vigil, an Amnesty International letter-writing campaign, and social justice volunteer opportunities galore—none of which need involve us in the incredibly embarrassing and countercultural act of getting involved with a Christian religious institution. It is so hard for Xers to connect with church that you can pretty much count on the fact that if we're there, it's because we want something not so easily found anywhere else: a living God and a spiritual community.

I am not sure that someone born before the 1960s can grasp how truly post-Christian our generation's experience has been, or how negative are most of our associations with the institutional church. *Clergy*: the word means "pedophiles." It means Jimmy Swaggart sweating into the TV cameras, moaning "I have sinned." It means the droning, oily-haired Reverend Lovejoy on *The Simpsons*. *Church*: it means hypocrisy. It means irrelevance. It means right-wing voting guides from the Christian Coalition. It is associated with pathetic environments like the lame local-access cable show to which Jesus Christ himself is relegated on the ineffable *South Park*. If we have normal friends our own age (and as Xer clergy we definitely may not) they probably neither go to church nor comprehend why we do. Believe me: if we clear these many hurdles and actually show up, we have got to want God pretty bad. I did.

Another place in which I feel this kind of discontinuity is in Episcopal efforts—and I cannot even think this phrase without mental, and rather arch, quotation marks—to "reach the youth." Ask for something "contemporary," and the Episcopal Church's default setting seems to be to downplay both the spiritual and Christianity's distinctiveness. We'll just have ski weekends and social events for the young adult fellowship, says the parish Christian education coordinator; they won't relate to anything religious. Surely the college group would be more interested in going to movies than in Bible study. Send those high-schoolers out for pizza quick.[8]

Unfortunately, for Xers, this strategy is backward. Postmodernism has led us to expect that each human tribe will have its distinctive worldview and way of life; tell us there's nothing special about yours and we'll stop caring fast.[9] Postmodernism has also led us to assume the reality of the spiritual, so that we are usually drawn in, not repelled, by mystery and the numinous—as long as it doesn't come off as manipulative.

Thus our current culture can find ancient, explicitly Christ-centered expressions of theology and liturgy strikingly relevant and fascinating. That which is uniquely Christian about Christianity stands the best chance of making Christianity uniquely meaningful to Xers—which makes the kind of baby-out-with-the-bathwater, meet-me-on-the-picket-line ministry that got so much press in the '60s and '70s an especially bad idea now.[10] On the West Coast, nondenominational churches designed for my generation are packing us in with incense, chants, and the unapologetic gospel of Jesus. Christian Xer magazines are reprinting the church fathers.[11] Some Episcopal churches are said to be making the postmodern turn as well—at least I hear anecdotes and rumors to that effect, although I have had little opportunity to check them out. However, I suspect such parishes are still in the minority; at one liturgy I attended last year, someone's idea of a "contemporary" recessional was an old protest song by Bob Dylan.

While I recognize that minimizing anything that would set Christians apart was at one point an important step in loosening up a powerful and entrenched religious institution, these days young adults have had it with letting the world dictate to the church. It strikes many of us as a sellout, plain and simple. On the other hand, we respect deeply the invitation to "plunge into the very core and heart of our faith."[12] "More worship," "we want to see Jesus," "show us the ancient paths"—these are the heart-cries of many postmodernists seeking God in Christ. Those have been my heart-cries for some time; for awhile I thought they were anti-contemporary and that I was very conservative and old-fashioned. I've come to see that they are actually where I am most cutting-edge.

The sense of discontinuity also arises whenever I encounter the climate of polarization that rules our denomination. In fact, perhaps the most stunning thing about the "Gathering the NeXt Generation" conference was the absence of that climate; everyone easily accepted and honored differences of opinion. Many Episcopalians seem to thrive on infighting, but it alienates and drains me. I fill up with despair at a clergy gathering as people tear apart a priest from across the diocese to whom they've never spoken but who represents some currently unfashionable position. I am left speechless as I watch the conversation on an Internet discussion list degenerate into name-calling within twenty-four hours of the 1998 Lambeth vote on sexuality. My stomach turns when I hear a layman name a seminary and say he wishes it would burn to the ground.[13]

It happens in so many places: the letters to the editor in *Episcopal Life*, the debates at diocesan conventions. I can only guess that people who choose to act this way believe vicious argument over hot-button issues is worth it.

But it's a belief that assumes that the Episcopal Church still has time, energy, money, members, and public goodwill to burn—as if we can squander as much of them as we like on attacking each other and suffer almost no consequences.

Yet aren't the consequences already staring us in the face? The way the church has allowed negativity to co-opt much of its public and media profile has deeply damaged Christianity's credibility.[14] A strong message has come across to Xers that Christians are people who oppose things, people, and behaviors, who are always repeating the deadly refrain of "we're against that." When we sign on to online spirituality message boards, we are used to seeing threads with titles like, "Why are Christians so *mean*?" We don't care if you're yelling because you oppose blessing of same-sex relationships or because you favor it; what we notice is the yelling. "With a postmodern mind-set, [Xers] process truth relationally," write Tim Celek and Dieter Zander in *Inside the Soul of a New Generation*.[15] If the church cannot demonstrate loving relationships in community, we will not bother with anything it says.

Another source of discontinuity for me is the value the Episcopal Church places on its own internal business systems. A clergy colleague was recently lamenting to me that almost no one under the age of fifty attended his parish's annual meetings; I suspect similar statistics apply to many of our several governance structures. The proposed solutions are predictable: appoint a youth representative to the standing committee, offer free diocesan training for vestry members, allow college chaplaincies voice and vote in convention. And, given our current structure, these courses of action are much better than doing nothing.

But as an Xer I am beginning to ask: why this obsession with governance in the first place?[16] Why all this energy toward maintenance of an institution? When clergy find an interested, spiritually alert parishioner, they invariably try to get her to participate in internal governance, whether through convention or vestry or diocesan committees or as a delegate to any number of in-house issue-oriented groups. Those slots seemingly have to get filled first, before anyone feels free to say, "I wonder whom we could ask to start networking with the housing project down the street?" or "Could we round up enough people to form a corps of lay visitors for evangelism?" And before someone runs to check my file, yes, I dutifully sign people up year after year and mail their names to the diocesan office. But I find it difficult to perceive the kingdom value in recruiting people for these roles and am always baffled when someone really covets one of them.[17]

The tolerance for using up much of our lay talent on governance seems to me to depend on assumptions similar to those supporting tolerance for political attacks. Where do we get the idea that we have the luxury in a post-Christian society of channeling our energy into such pursuits? In a world that does not know Christ, is it really important to emphasize keeping internal committees fully staffed? The words of Jerome speak directly to our time: "While sin reigns, we build cities for the Egyptians. . . . [W]e seek chaff instead of grain and structures of mud instead of solid rock."[18]

To me, it seems crucial in a post-Christian context to shift energy and emphasis to that solid rock and that nourishing grain. It is crucial to get off the governance treadmill. Apart from a small group genuinely needed (and, one hopes, spiritually gifted and called) for administration, why can't the majority of lay energy be plugged into encountering the living God and doing ministry where it's needed most?

Most of the examples of discontinuity I have mentioned are tied to and exacerbated by a larger issue, about which much has been written. Along with other old-line denominations, the Episcopal Church seems to take for granted our society's general acceptance of Christianity. The way we do business assumes the context of what has been called Christendom.[19] Despite several years of discussions about moving into a post-Christian era, our corporate behavior remains rooted in a sense of the Christian church as a privileged Western institution with a special role in public life, whose opinions will be respected and whose professional employees have an obligation to service the general society with appropriate sacraments, rites, political interventions, and public policy statements.

I know from history books that this enduring "sense" once corresponded to reality; but it is a reality I have never experienced, because Christendom is, of course, dead. But you wouldn't know it from looking at us. Most of the Episcopal Church's active clergy grew up and have done the majority of their ministry in Christendom, and almost all the parishes I know run on a Christendom-based model. "The shells of the old structures surround us even though many of them no longer work," writes Loren Mead.[20] And how could they work, when the social context to which they were tailored is extinct? But still these old structures set the parameters for our activity; they have a subtle and coercive veto power, and you cannot step far outside them without having a pejorative label slapped on you. And yet, as a member of the first generation in the church to have lived exclusively after Christendom, I find myself tripping every day over the shells of those persistent, nonworking structures.

For example, I am genuinely baffled by phone calls from long-inactive parishioners who see it as the church's duty to provide weddings and baptisms to their agnostic descendants. Similarly, I feel at sea trying to assist in

an inquirers' class that presumes previously unchurched attendees already
know all about Christianity and just need a tour of Anglican history and customs. I have, of course, learned how to navigate in this Christendom-based
environment, but it will never be native territory to me. I simply do not know
what it would mean to think of the church or of Christianity as privileged,
public, or normative. Nor do I know what it would mean to take for granted
that most people in America are already Christians. Christianity gets one link
on "Yahoo: Faiths and Practices," the same as paganism, Tenrikyo, and
Santeria.[21]

As I think of how all these discontinuities conspire to keep my generation out of the church, that image has become the most evocative: the Xer
with mouse poised, contemplating the next step in a virtual journey. Postmodern to the bones, s/he is open to the supernatural and craving distinctive spiritual community. As the pointer slides across the screen and selects
one underlined word, s/he is thinking: OK, Christianity, show me some
added value—and the damn link had better work, and whatever it points to
had better relate to what you say the center of your life is—*that would be Jesus,
wouldn't it?*—rather than giving me pop psychology, the schedule for a buildings and grounds committee, or a list of people being denounced by one of
your zillion arguing denominations—or I'm clicking somewhere else.

Although I know the feeling, I myself am not that Xer. I have already
clicked. I have committed my life to serving Jesus Christ through the Episcopal
Church. While I feel the discontinuities sharply, there is still nowhere I would
rather be. My commitment has only increased since attending GTNG, which
I left filled with hope about what Xers have to offer to the future of our
denomination. But that offering cannot be effective until it is accepted. While
I have watched my Episcopal Church learn to accept other outsider voices by
listening seriously to the account they give of their experience, so far I find
many people surprisingly unwilling to believe Xers when we speak. The
question I ask day after day is: Will the church choose to hear us soon
enough, and well enough, that we can help keep the rest of our peer group
from clicking somewhere else?

NOTES

1. While I find a sense of humor in general to be highly valued in Episcopal
   churches, here I refer to irony as a primary means of grappling with and
   communicating religious claims themselves. *In Virtual Faith: The Irreverent
   Spiritual Quest of Generation X* (San Francisco: Jossey-Bass, 1998), Tom
   Beaudoin argues that the use of irony is fundamental to the culture of vir-

tuality that underlies Generation X's interaction with religion. "Irony on the part of Xers is a way of marking distance from what is received as religious in order to collapse that religiousness playfully, to iron(ize) it flat. Then, through pop culture, Xers suggest something else in its place. . . . To operate ironically, as GenX pop culture does, is not merely to take a negative, dismissive tone. It is to engage for the sake of reclamation—but only after the devastation of an engagement that destroys" (41).

2. Lutheran theologian Philip Melanchthon (1497–1560) used the Greek word *adiaphora* (lit., "things indifferent") to refer to practices neither specifically commanded nor specifically forbidden by scripture. Since *adiaphora* are not essential to the faith, they may be altered as circumstances demand. Defining the term *adiaphora* is often much easier for Christians than agreeing on whether some particular thing is or is not an example of it.

3. Catechism, *BCP* 855.

4. Two examples are the Web site of Mars Hill Fellowship in Seattle (www.marshillchurch.org) and the advertisements on CD from Michael Slaughter's *Out on the Edge: A Wake-Up Call for Church Leaders on the Edge of the Media Reformation* (Nashville: Abingdon Press, 1998).

5. Kevin Graham Ford, *Jesus for a New Generation* (Downers Grove, Ill.: InterVarsity Press, 1995), 31.

6. I owe the phrasing of this insight to Theron Walker, who presented the idea in his GTNG workshop, "Tradition in Post-Christendom: It's Not Just for Tevye Anymore." He in turn credits Stanley Hauerwas and William H. Willimon's *Resident Aliens* (Nashville: Abingdon Press, 1989), which bluntly suggests that "few books have been a greater hindrance to an accurate assessment of our situation than *Christ and Culture*" (40).

7. Not to mention imperialistic. After a sermon I preached on "What Is a Christian?" one person came to me with this definition, penned by a friend from a late-1960s church political group: "A Christian is someone who gives a damn." The unthinking arrogance of that sentence leaves me breathless. Atheists give a damn. Buddhists give a damn. Lots of people give a damn. Who do we think we are?

8. This "default setting" points to youth and young adult ministry that is still geared for a Baby-Boomer context, even twenty years after the last Boomers entered college. In the next paragraphs, I will be speaking of what an Xer-oriented ministry could look like. However, if the birth dates of 1961–81 prove to be correct, the last Xers graduated from high school in 1999. Our chief focus in youth ministry now ought to be designing programs geared for the Millennial generation, who may or may not react the way Xers tend to react.

9. Stanley Grenz explains, "The [postmodern] conviction that each person is embedded in a particular human community leads to a corporate understanding of truth. . . . Postmoderns live in self-contained social groups, each of which has its own language, beliefs, and values. . . . Beliefs are held to be true within the context of the communities that espouse them" (*A Primer on Postmodernism* [Grand Rapids, Mich.: Eerdmans, 1996], 14–15).

10. Beaudoin makes a similar point in *Virtual Faith*: "A Methodist colleague who took his young adult group to a monastery and read mystical works with them told me that he had been hounded ever since with requests to return; he dryly compared this with the lack of requests to repeat a recent young adult worship service his church had sponsored" (165).

    The same kind of disconnect occurs in one-on-one "reach the youth" efforts. One afternoon, a fellow (though younger and more stereotypical) Generation Xer and I happened to run into a Boomer priest I knew. In our conversation, the priest found opportunities to make several sarcastic and self-consciously secular comments, seasoning them liberally with profanity. After he left, my unchurched companion incredulously and pityingly hit the nail on the head: "He was trying to impress me, wasn't he?" I had to admit it was true; that was the man's idea of a contemporary evangelistic strategy.

11. Two examples of Xer magazines that often draw on patristics are *Beyond*, online at www.beyondmag.com, and *re:generation quarterly*, online at www.regenerator.com.

12. William Mahedy and Janet Bernardi, *A Generation Alone: Xers Making a Place in the World* (Downers Grove, Ill.: InterVarsity Press, 1994), 65.

13. No, I won't tell you which one.

14. This problem is not unique to the Episcopal Church. Presbyterians and United Methodists have had well-publicized battles, and preachers outside the mainline denominations seem to find plenty to denounce. In whatever setting, the last exclamation one is likely to hear would be the one to which Tertullian refers in chapter 39 of his *Apology*: "See how these Christians love one another!"

15. Tim Celek and Dieter Zander, *Inside the Soul of a New Generation* (Grand Rapids, Mich.: Zondervan, 1996), 114.

16. The book that framed this issue for me was Thomas J. Bandy's *Breaking Habits: Welcome Relief for Addicted Churches* (Nashville: Abingdon Press, 1997). The first two chapters are invaluable for unmasking the declining church's obsession with governance.

17. It seems especially ironic that our denomination strives to recruit for governance slots, while actively resisting recruitment for ordained ministry.

18. Quoted in Christopher A. Hall, *Reading Scripture with the Church Fathers* (Downers Grove, Ill.: InterVarsity Press, 1998), 112.
19. The best-known current work on this topic is Loren Mead, *The Once and Future Church* (Washington, D.C.: Alban Institute, 1991). Essentially a work of ecclesiology, Mead's book is neither a restatement of the argument that the church should adapt to a culture that has become secularized nor a reminder that America has no officially "established" religion. It calls for a reinvention of the congregation in light of the new mission frontier at our doorstep.
20. Ibid., 43.
21. In this regard, the postmodern climate bears a striking resemblance to the pre-Constantinian climate. In both cases, the surrounding culture is full of religious options, yet largely ignorant of (or intermittently hostile to) the church. The Web page to which I refer is part of the Yahoo! directory, located at http://dir.yahoo.com/Society_and_Culture/Religion_and_Spirituality/Faiths_and_Practices/

To Be Young, Priested, and Black

Raising Up the NeXt Generation of Black Clergy

Jennifer Lynn Baskerville

Statistics are funny things. They can paint broad strokes of a portrait, and they can be massaged and molded to mean just about anything. They can shed light on a truth or twist reality beyond all recognition. They are very powerful. Two statistics have captured and held my imagination over the past several years.

On May 23, 1997, the day I graduated from seminary, an African American female priest—a mentor of mine—passed on a reality-checking statistic. Out of some eight thousand active clergy in the Episcopal Church, fewer than thirty were African American women serving in full-time parish ministry. In a few short weeks I was to become one of them.

Almost one year later I would hear the second statistic. According to the Church Pension Fund, out of some eight thousand active clergy in the Episcopal Church, fewer than three hundred are thirty-five and younger. Fewer than ten of these young clergy are of African descent. I am one of them. These two statistics do indeed paint a few broad strokes on the portrait that is the Episcopal Church, and they shed light on a truth about who we are as opposed to who we would like to say we are. These statistics hold power not just for me as a young, Black priest of Generation X, but they affect all of us who love and hold claim to the Episcopal Church.

There is no doubt that the dearth of young Black clergy is a concern to Episcopalians of African descent. The view ten and twenty years down the road points to a future with relatively few Black clergy. After serving long and distinguished tenures, bishops and priests of African descent are retiring at a rapid rate, prompting the question from where the next generation of Black bishops will come. In a time in which an astoundingly high proportion of Black role models comes from the sports and entertainment industries, Blacks in the church struggle to find accessible, approachable, and Christ-centered role models for the youth of Black America. The Black lay leadership of our church attempts to meet this great need with dedication and purpose.

However, there is the recognition that Black clergy, working alongside the laity, have a particular role to play in the lives of our young people. Lastly, as the young Anglo clergy of Generation X seeks to speak, reach out to, and serve those members of Generation X both inside and outside the church, the Black church is seeking to do the same for the hip-hop generation that stands inside and outside the doors. The Old Testament lament, "Who will go for us?" takes on a new urgency for the Black community of the Episcopal Church.

Who will go for us, indeed. The "us," however, is not just the "us" of the Black community, but it is the collective "us" of the whole people of God. Episcopalians of African descent do not exist in a vacuum. We mirror and help compose the larger picture of the Episcopal Church. Though circumstances of race, history, and culture serve to coalesce the Black community and create a shared, but by no means monolithic, identity, the fact remains (thanks be to God!) that Black Episcopalians are part of the larger whole and help to make the whole what it is. Therefore, I would suggest that the dearth of young Black clergy is a concern not just for Black Episcopalians alone, but that it is a concern to the Episcopal Church as a whole.

In the pages that follow it is my intent to examine the call-and-discernment process of young, Black clergy in the Episcopal Church. I begin by laying out a theological construct for calling and ordaining men and women from a variety of backgrounds; I then link that framework to our current situation. After profiling the ordination process of three Black priests, I conclude with some reflections and recommendations for those who have interest, involvement, and oversight of ordination processes as to how we might make these processes more inviting, pastoral, and healthy for aspirants of all races and backgrounds.

My viewpoint is rooted in an understanding of the *imago Dei*, the image of God. In the creation narrative in the first chapter of Genesis, God completes the work of calming the chaos and of creating all living things—plants and animals—and then decides to create humankind. Verse 26 says, "Then God said, 'Let us make humankind in our image, according to our likeness. . . .'" When I look around and see the diversity of humankind I have no doubt in my mind that the image of God is complex. There have been many interpretations of the *imago Dei* throughout Christian tradition. These interpretations, to name a few, have found the human reflection of the divine in physical resemblance, in the capacity to reason, and in the power to exercise dominion over creation. A more modern view contends that the image of God describes "human life in relationship."[1] This construction sees God's image not as a set of physical or intellectual attributes but places God's image in the realm of transcendence of self in relationship. God in the Holy Trinity exhibits perfect relationship in community. By creating humanity not as a solitary state but as an existence which from its very beginnings is relational ("male and female he created them"), God establishes that to be created in God's image means to be in relationship.

The fullness of God's image is not found in discrete, compartmentalized existence. The full image of God is beyond our knowing. However, I do not believe it is possible even to glimpse the image of God without taking into account the complexity and variety of humanity. To discount a section of humanity is to discount the fullness of God. Therefore, we find ourselves on shaky ground relationally and theologically to divide the church of God—God's human family—into discrete compartments that are not wholly connected and whose lives have no impact upon one another. For instance, we are denigrating the image of God when homeless individuals and their problems are treated as though they had no impact on the middle class. It is the full family of God that reflects God's image, and some of us are Black, some Asian, some Eastern European, some rich, some poor. We are all in this together.

Having few clergy of African descent not only deprives the Black community of a richly diverse clerical leadership, it deprives the entire church of that gift. Without people of color, or the deaf, or Latinos, or any of the others often pushed to the margins of society, we lose the complexity of voices longing to share stories that have gone untold. And when the stories go untold we, as a church, never fully understand who we are.

Appreciating the fullness of God's image is foundational. The case for raising up more young clergy of African descent could easily be made on the grounds of correcting the imbalances and injustices wrought by our common heritage of slavery and the persistence of racism and class prejudice. To be sure, these remain issues for our church community to confront, engage, and eradicate. However, I subscribe to the belief that all the antiracism work is for naught unless we understand our basic relationship to God and to one another, and our connectedness through Christ. We cannot all be one in Christ Jesus if some are part of the image of God and others are not.

How, then, are we to reconcile the promise that the image of God holds for us as a church with the sobering statistics with which this essay began? The issue is two-sided, of course. On the one hand is the challenge of attracting young Black men and women to the idea of serving God as a priest. On the other is the challenge of making the call and ordination process truly one of discernment and support for all who would aspire to answer God's call, and that would also be open to the diversity of people and experience that God often calls to serve the church.

As I mentioned at the outset, one of the most enlightening ways of getting the sense of a picture is seeing as many pieces as possible. A half-dozen Black clergy were surveyed for this essay about their call-and-discernment process. In what follows I share the stories of the ordination process as experienced by two young Black clergy, Reginald Payne-Wiens and me, and by one clergyperson—Gayle Harris—who, although older now, was ordained young. The stories they tell are shaped and defined by the churches and dioceses that presented them for ordination as well as by the dates in which they were in process. However, the stories all work together to show how the call-and-ordination process has changed for Blacks in the Episcopal Church over the years, as well as to point to the areas of challenge and support that have remained consistent. More important, I hope that the possibilities for creating healthy and supportive structures for ordination discernment will become clear.

While there are a number of predominantly Black Episcopal congregations, such as St. James' in Baltimore and the Church of the Intercession in Harlem, which are known for raising up clergy, the call and ordination of Black clergy yields many different experiences. It isn't always the case, for example, that Black clergy are sponsored by predominantly Black congregations. And there is no typical profile or process for the young, Black ordination candidate. However, because I interviewed priests who were ordained in their twenties or early thirties, the stories share some similarities.

Of those interviewed, the average time spent in the ordination process—from the first visit to a priest expressing the desire to enter a process of discernment to the date of ordination to the diaconate—was six to seven years. In almost every case there was a break or intermediate stop before the process was completed. For some this break allowed for the completion of undergraduate education or the pursuit of an additional graduate degree. For others, the break was imposed to allow the young aspirant time to gain "experience in the world." Unsurprisingly, another similarity shared by those interviewed was the financial strain that the ordination process and seminary education can bring. On the positive side, those interviewed had networks of support both within and outside the ordination process that allowed them to continue even under the most trying circumstances.

The Reverend Gayle Harris is one of the early pioneers of Black women clergy in the Episcopal Church, and as such she has helped pave the way for the current generation of young Black clergy. Ordained to the priesthood on February 11, 1982, Harris was only the sixth Black woman to be ordained priest in the Episcopal Church. She was thirty-one years old. During the seven years she was in the ordination process, from 1975–82, Harris encountered the usual hoops and obstacles, but there were different dynamics at work. Telling of the period, Harris said that none of these dynamics was related to age. Most seminarians in the ordination process were in their late twenties and early thirties. But in 1975, when she first began to think seriously about a call to ordained ministry, ordination to the priesthood was not an option for women. When in 1977 she got more serious about ordination, she found herself in a diocese (Chicago) that would ordain women only to the diaconate. Race was also an issue. Harris recalls that it was as if there were a door marked for ordination, and it said, "White men only," and, "Colored men to the back." It was as if there were no door for women, let alone Black women. Nevertheless, in 1978 Harris entered the Church Divinity School of the Pacific as a postulant from the Diocese of Chicago.

Throughout her process Harris had a mentor in Bishop Quentin Primo. In fact, whenever she met with Bishop James Montgomery—then diocesan bishop of Chicago—Primo was always present. Primo, who was Black, was a great source of support and guidance. Harris would be ordained to the diaconate in Chicago, but it was made clear that she was to seek ministry opportunities elsewhere. Bishop Montgomery wanted to help her find a church, and Harris found herself in the Diocese of Newark at Grace, Van Vorst, in Jersey City. She thought that she would transfer to Newark to complete her ordination process and then transfer back to Chicago. But that never happened. Instead she would serve in the Dioceses of Maryland, Washington, D.C., and Rochester, New York, where she now serves as a rector.

Having settled in the Diocese of Newark, Harris found her process of ordination to be fraught with its own difficulties. The ordination of women to the priesthood was still a novel idea, and not all dioceses and bishops were supportive of the concept, although they were often supportive of the women. That was the case for Bishop Montgomery, who offered Harris great support but was not willing to ordain women. Other dioceses that were accepting of women's ordination often became revolving doors for women seeking ordination. The Diocese of Newark was trying not to be one of them.

Once in Newark, Harris found herself without all of the support she had relied on in Chicago. The Commission on Ministry of Newark did not know her and yet were charged with approving her (or not) for ordination. In their brief ten-minute meetings Harris recalls that there was little opportunity to develop a relationship with the commission members. There were no mentors or liaisons in the diocese to guide her through the rest of the process. She felt that she was not taken seriously. The process was a tough one, but Harris would indeed be ordained to the priesthood in the Diocese of Newark. She currently serves as rector of St. Luke and Simon Cyrene Episcopal Church in Rochester, New York.

Like many who go through the ordination process, Harris understood the importance of a network of friends and colleagues that could offer support. In addition to the bishops who supported her, she found great encouragement from the Union of Black Episcopalians and the network of Black clergy. "Being able to call [now Bishop] Barbara Harris on the phone and having folks who were a generation ahead and older folks whose shoulder I could cry on" was an essential part of her support system. And as one of the first six Black women ordained to the priesthood in the Episcopal Church, Harris was part of a unique and tight circle of friendship and support. "We were always there for each other," Harris says. "Phones and jets made everything possible.... Nan Peete, Barbara Harris, Ann Redding—they are still my closest friends."

Reflecting on her experience, Harris finds that being Black and female in the ordination process had its most profound implication in deployment. She remembers her final year of seminary as especially difficult, because by graduation most of her classmates had jobs while she was still trying to get interviews. In those days, being hired by a predominantly White congregation was simply not an option. If she could change anything about the ordination process, Harris would create more diversity in fieldwork placements. She would encourage White seminarians to go to Black parishes, and vice versa. "It would open up the doors of experience and expectation—to see what is possible." That is one of the keys to opening up the ordination process to young people of all colors. It is important to see what is possible—to look up to the chancel and to think, yes, God might even call someone such as myself to serve.

Nearly twenty years since Harris was in seminary, the ordination process and deployment outlook for young Black postulants and clergy in some ways have changed. In almost all dioceses the ordination of women to the priesthood has ceased to be a major issue. Currently, age is more apt to be a factor than gender. In deployment, Black clergy regularly serve as curates or assistants in predominantly White parishes. There are, by and large, fewer overt obstacles to the process for young Black men and women, but obstacles do still exist.

◄○►

The Reverend Reginald Payne-Wiens, currently associate at St. Paul's Episcopal Church in Paterson, New Jersey, was ordained to the priesthood on June 6, 1998, after seven years in the process. He was thirty years old. When he thinks about the major obstacles he encountered, Payne-Wiens without hesitation cites age and economic background. Payne-Wiens experienced a call to ordained ministry while in college but was told to take a year to work in the "real world" before going further. In addition, he found himself tripped up over culture and class issues and the accompanying expectations. This didn't delay the process—just three months on the way to candidacy—as much as it made it more difficult to maneuver within the process. Having grown up in rural Georgia, Payne-Wiens understood that he needed to be especially savvy.

Payne-Wiens, a 1997 graduate of Virginia Theological Seminary, had a unique situation during his ordination process. He was sponsored for ordination by a bishop who had been his rector. Bishop Henry Louttit, Jr., was elected in the Diocese of Georgia when Payne-Wiens was in the middle of the process. This aroused concern from some quarters over whether the bishop's support was genuine or a political ploy of some sort. In addition, one-third of the Commission on Ministry was from his sponsoring parish—all but two knew him from his work as a counselor at the diocesan camp.

Payne-Wiens would find great support from the bishop but found that, without a rector, an immediate source of support and mentoring was missing. The end of the process was a very lonely one for Payne-Wiens, and he wishes that he had had a mentor—particularly a seasoned Black priest to help him navigate the sometimes murky waters. A clear and strong support system is what Payne-Wiens cites as the key element missing from his experience. Moreover, Payne-Wiens had been made a postulant for ordination three years before he entered seminary. Although he met with the Commission on Ministry at the beginning of the process, he would not see them again until four years later, when he was interviewed for candidacy. By that time, membership of the commission had almost completely turned over. There was no formal discernment committee and no liaison to the Commission on Ministry. Indeed, there was very little communication, and Payne-Wiens experienced a sense of abandonment from the diocesan structure. Throughout that time he relied on his home parish, friends throughout his diocese, and Black students at Virginia Theological Seminary and at other seminaries for support. If he could make one change in his process it would be to create a formal support structure. Since Payne-Wiens's ordination an E-mail connection between persons in process has been established.

Other young Black clergy with whom I spoke had positive experiences in their discernment and ordination processes. These included the Reverend Theodora Brooks, a Liberian woman serving in the Diocese of New York, who, at twenty-six, was the first woman to be ordained from her diocese; and the Reverend John Thompson-Quartey, a native of Ghana recently called to serve as a chaplain at St. Paul's School in New Hampshire. It is, perhaps, too easy and somewhat misleading to paint a picture of the ordination process for young Black clergy by concentrating on those who have been ordained. For every Black priest there are several young men and women who struggle to get into a diocesan ordination process but who are hindered by financial constraints, inadequate resources at the parish level, and the subtle and not-so-subtle dynamics of race. Once in the process, a new struggle begins: paying for the ever-escalating costs of a seminary education, meeting the often overly cumbersome ordination requirements, and learning to speak the languages of both the White and the Black church fluently. The struggle is undertaken with the understanding that ordination is not guaranteed until the bishop's hands are laid upon one's head. It is a wonder that anyone would enter such a daunting process. And yet, for the few Black men and women who seek to offer their lives in service to the church, ten or more years may pass before they find themselves kneeling before a bishop at an ordination service.

This was certainly the picture with which I was presented when I first began to voice my sense of call to ordained ministry—and for good reason. This was the reality many of my Black brothers and sisters had lived through. However, when I think about my ordination process I am pretty clear that I would not change a thing. It was by no means perfect, but it was as healthy and supportive as I would have wanted it to be. I reflect on it to help highlight what I believe are some of the key elements to attracting and supporting young men and women—of any color—through the ordination process.

I was ordained to the priesthood on February 7, 1998, about eight years after giving any real thought to serving the church as a priest. I was twenty-four years old, just a few years out of college, when I first thought about ordained ministry. I was living in New York City—where I was born and raised—working for a regional planning think tank and becoming increasingly involved in the life of Trinity Church at Wall Street. Although I was active in several ministries, including cofacilitating adult confirmation classes, writing for the newsletter, and serving on the parish congregational council, it was while working to create a young adult ministry that a sense of call began to emerge. At one of our frequent young adult planning meetings a priest asked me if I had ever considered ordained ministry. As it turned out, I had given it some thought but until that night had yet to give utterance to my struggle with a sense of call. The priest who asked me to consider ordination was the curate, Caroline Stacey, a twenty-seven-year-old White woman from England who had been ordained priest at Trinity at a wonderful Sunday morning liturgy the year before. That she was a young adult woman was not insignificant. Here was a person at the same stage of life inviting me to consider the rather radical idea of discerning ordination. Had the invitation come from a sixty-year-old man I would not have taken it less seriously, but this female young adult broadened my picture of the possible. If she could discern ordination, then my discernment was not as crazy an idea as I initially thought.

At this point in my life I had already been blessed with a rich array of images of priestly ministry. I had not attended the Episcopal Church until college, in 1984. At the local church in Northampton, Massachusetts, there were men and women clergy on staff. When I arrived at Trinity/Wall Street four years later, the priests on staff were male and female, Black and White, old and young. In my naïveté, I thought it had always been that way. I later learned that such a clergy mix was the result of a long process of change and struggle in the national church—a process that continues even now. I was blessed, though, to know a diversity of clergy not as a possibility but as an accepted reality that I assumed was part of the typical Episcopal experience.

It would be several more months before I felt ready to meet with Canon Lloyd Casson, then the vicar of Trinity Church, to discuss the discernment process. Some of that had to do with my own reticence, but much of it was related to the "war stories" I had heard from other clergy and the notes of discouragement often innocently given by laity. "Why would you want to be a priest? You could be a great architect!" "Why bother with the [ordination] process? Do you know how much time and money it will take?" "There aren't any jobs for priests, stay where you are. Go do something else first and then talk about it when you have had some more experience." This is much of what I heard before I even darkened the vicar's door! Where were the words of joy and support? I thought this was a wonderful adventure on which I was about to embark. Reality checks were fine—I sought those out. But the discouragement was more than I bargained for. In the end, it was the words of the curate, of several close friends, and of what I discerned to be the voice of God that pushed me at least to talk about the possibility of a call with someone who might help me to sort it out.

There was another reason I waited. I already had a vocation planned, and this sense of call to ministry was rocking what I thought was the very steady boat of a career in architectural preservation. I had majored in architecture in college, and after nearly four years in the fields of historic preservation and urban planning, working as a preservationist was as real a vocation to me as a call to ordained ministry. My discernment with Lloyd Casson and with several priests involved in religious art and architecture helped to bring some clarity to my emerging call. Perhaps God was calling me to be a priest and a historic preservationist who worked to restore religious properties!

I ended up attending Cornell University, where I earned my graduate degree in preservation. I was now living in Ithaca, and older and wiser voices convinced me that it was best to enter the ordination process in the diocese in which I was physically resident, Central New York. The Episcopal Church at Cornell had been my church home while in Ithaca, and it became the natural place to seek sponsorship for ordination. And so I began all over again, meeting with the parish discernment committee and the Reverend Gurdon Brewster, the chaplain, to further discern this call. I have always believed strongly in a call consisting of three components: personal call, community call, and God's call. For me, an authentic call had to be affirmed by all three. So it was important to become a part of the community at Cornell and to honor the full process of discernment in that place.

I was surprised, however, by the feedback I received from those expecting me to be sponsored by a Black congregation. It was as though it were not possible for a Black woman to be sponsored by a predominantly White congregation. Some, White and Black alike, wondered if I would be hampered by not having had the Black experience. There were no Black congregations in the Diocese of Central New York. Did this matter? Would I be any less legitimate? Did my race really need to dictate my ordination process? As many in the ordination process have discovered, it is easy to be caught in the middle of expectations based on the way things used to be and of hopeful expectations of the way things might be. Then, as now, I felt there was no room for that kind of nit-picking.

The process at Trinity/Wall Street and at the Episcopal Church at Cornell that led to my ordination was a good one. The Commission on Ministry chair explained at our first meeting that the Diocese of Central New York had recently reworked the ordination process so that it would adapt to the needs of the particular aspirant. The process operated within the boundaries of church canons, but the Commission on Ministry did not fit all aspirants into the same cookie-cutter mold. Being young was not a liability. Furthermore, the bishop, David Joslin, seemed to relish the raising up of younger vocations. At one point, three of us in the process were under thirty, fairly remarkable considering the small-town nature of the diocese.

Several other factors made the ordination process healthy. Communication between all postulants, candidates, and deacons and the Commission on Ministry was encouraged, and structures were put in place to make that communication happen. For instance, yearly meetings with members of the commission and, toward the end of the process, the Standing Committee enabled these committees to get to know those in the ordination process, and those in the process were able to get to know one another. Thus a community of active discernment was formed. This community of support existed alongside other support systems. The seminary community at the Church

Divinity School of the Pacific in Berkeley, California, was a dynamic place of learning, but it also was a source of encouragement and support. Living three thousand miles from my home in New York made a positive seminary experience crucial. And like all the other priests profiled in this essay, the Black community was essential for providing friendship and mentors. Some of these mentors were older, seasoned priests who had seen it all and survived. People like Nan Peete took the role of mentoring seriously and actively reached out to lend support and friendship. Other friendships and opportunities for leadership through the Union of Black Episcopalians and the Organization of Black Episcopal Seminarians were significant in shaping my ministerial identity. For years these organizations have served this role for dozens of Blacks in the ordination process.

I found these networks all the more important as a candidate in a predominantly White diocese in which I would be the only priest of color, although two others joined the diocese later. It was important for me to see the full display of possible images—to see and experience the variety of gifts that the Black church contributes to the Episcopal Church as a whole.

This full and colorful portrait should be a primary feature in a church that seeks to reflect, as best as possible, the image of God. Clearly, the call and ordination of young Black clergy will need to rely not just on images but on concrete realities. In conclusion I share some thoughts on the three areas—mentoring relationships, financial feasibility, and vocational perception—in which the church may make an immediate impact on the ordination process for young aspirants of African descent. In the end, however, I believe these recommendations will increase the numbers of young aspirants regardless of race.

MENTORING RELATIONSHIPS

One of the truths that rings clear from those interviewed for this essay is the importance of having healthy and stable mentors at each stage of the ordination process. Those seeking ordination—particularly young adults—will find themselves where few of their friends and colleagues have gone. Hordes of young men and women can gather to discuss the rigors of business school; seasoned veterans of the business world can be found by the thousands. Not so with the church. Few vocational choices can seem as isolating as the priesthood. This makes having colleagues and mentors all the more crucial. The web of the ordination process is complicated. It is all too easy to become ensnared and, in some cases, eaten alive. Over and over clergy cite the importance of having accessible role models to engage, savvy clergy to lend advice, and friends who have "been there" to offer a voice of sanity in what often seems like an insane venture.

As part of preparation for ordination many dioceses appoint liaisons or shepherds to persons in process. These liaisons—lay and ordained—are often great sources of information and channels of communication while a postulant or candidate is in seminary. Dioceses might also consider inviting clergy to serve as mentors to individuals throughout their process. Alternatively, dioceses might require persons in process to engage a mentor on their own but to be in communication with the Commission on Ministry or bishop from time to time about that relationship. Many persons in process will have a bevy of advisers and mentors, culled over time, with whom to consult during their long journey to ordination. But many do not. When sponsoring rectors leave congregations, for example, a crucial piece of the support structure may disappear, leaving candidates on their own. A more structured system of mentoring may help provide stable and ongoing guidance in what is often a tenuous undertaking.

FINANCIAL FEASIBILITY

Answering God's call to ordained ministry is an expensive proposition. The expense is also a successful deterrent to some of the most gifted aspirants. It is not unusual for postulants to sell their homes in order to finance the cost of seminary. Young adults do not usually have assets of that size, nor have they often saved large amounts of money through prior employment. While some scholarships are available through seminaries, churches, and church-related agencies, they rarely cover the full cost of seminary, which currently hovers around $25,000 annually for tuition, books, and living expenses.

In addition to the cost of attending seminary are the fees for psychological testing, psychiatric exams, physical exams before and after seminary, Clinical Pastoral Education, travel to and from meetings with the Commission on Ministry, and the opportunity costs lost in not having full-time employment during summer breaks. These add up quickly. It is not uncommon for the laying on of hands to be accompanied by the laying on of a $20,000 student-loan debt. And these expenses may all be added to preexisting debt remaining from undergraduate education.

A possible solution may exist in the creation of no-interest loans sponsored by the national church. These loans would provide financial assistance to future clergy while decreasing some of the debt burden on the newly ordained. Like federal education loans, these loans would require repayment within ten years of graduation from seminary—or perhaps even less time, given the absence of compounded interest. This loan program might be administered by an agency of the Episcopal Church such as the Church Pension Fund. The Presbyterian Church (USA) operates such a loan program and may provide a good model.

In a situation in which "every little bit helps," a no-interest loan would ease some of the financial strain of answering God's call to ordained ministry.

VOCATIONAL PERCEPTION

Lastly, an easy way to help make Black young adults more open to considering ordination would be changing the perception of the vocation. Many young men and women of African descent who experience a call are made hesitant by the "war stories" often told by Black and White clergy alike about their ordination process or experience in ministry. I have seen the negative perceptions about the vocation to ordained ministry send many talented young adults running to law school. Like my colleagues, I am often surprised by the reactions I receive when I say that I had a positive ordination process. It seems that for most people discerning ordination, the process is fraught with setbacks, difficulties, and disappointments. This is no less true if you are Black.

Indeed, because "war stories" have loomed so large among Black candidates for ordination through the years, a positive experience receives the respect usually granted a minor miracle. But the "war stories" are many, and they are true. One needs only to remember or read about the experience of Black clergy to see the depth of pain in the struggle to love and serve a church that was not clear about wanting your ministry. So we must respect our history. But to allow it to confine us would be a mistake. The positive stories and encouragement to enter this fulfilling vocation too often go unheard. The joy of serving God in this way too often goes unseen. My perception is that this reality is slowly changing, but it is incumbent on all clergy to provide a realistic picture of this call that includes the good and the bad.

An increase in vocations among Black young adults will require not only changes in vocational perception and financial burdens, and the addition of mentoring programs, but a necessary shift in the Episcopal Church. An increase in vocations requires that the church dare to see and welcome the diversity of race, background, and theological belief that makes up its beautiful, if sometimes uneasy, composition. It will call on the ability of the Episcopal Church to embrace the fullness of the image of God and to rejoice in those moments when the church itself reflects that image.

NOTES

1. See Daniel L. Migliore, *Faith Seeking Understanding* (Grand Rapids, Mich.: Eerdmans, 1991), 122.

Conversion and Community

Nancy A. Vogele

In 1988, as a twenty-four-year-old, I went to the other side of the world for two years to serve as a volunteer for mission in the Diocese of Shaba, Zaire.[1] Several months before leaving for Zaire, someone gave me a *National Geographic* map of Africa. I opened it up and looked at it. At the top of the map was Europe. I was surprised at how small it was. Just below all of Europe, however, was Africa. It was huge, taking up the rest of the large sheet. I thought to myself, "Nancy, you might have studied in France twice and traveled all over Europe, but you ain't seen nothing yet." That map was a visual symbol of the big, new adventure on which I was about to embark.

I went to Zaire because I wanted to go beyond where I had been: to leave the center and move to the edges of my reality. I truly wanted to be of service to others in the church whom I perceived needed it. I was young and somewhat naïve; I was very excited about going to Africa, and I looked at this experience as a kind of Christian Peace Corps.

I spent two incredible years working under the Right Reverend E. M. Kolini. My official title was youth worker, but I also helped organize the Sunday School program for the diocese. Additionally, I helped the bishop catch up and stay caught up with his English correspondence, and I completed and translated (from local Swahili to French) reports from the diocese's first-ever synod. I was even the driver when the diocesan driver did not show up. In short, I did what needed to be done—sometimes well and sometimes not so well.

During my time in Zaire, I experienced a profound conversion that can be illustrated by a few stories. Before I left for Zaire, I got it in my head that part of my mission was to give hope to the people I would be working with and serving. I thought, "God, how can I as a middle-class, white American who has never gone a day in her life without food or shelter, who has never experienced hardship of any kind—how on earth can I teach them about hope?"

Several months after arriving, I was worshiping one Sunday in a small and dynamic church. The sermon was rousing, the singing exuberant, the people dancing and singing and full of joy. All of a sudden, it was as if God whispered in my ear, "Oh, Nancy. I forgot to tell you. I didn't intend for you to teach these folks about hope. I meant for you to learn about hope from them!" My concept of mission turned on its head. Maybe God wasn't using me in these people's conversion. Maybe God was using them to convert me.

Another instrument of my conversion was a Zairian woman whom I passed on the road one day. I had been in Zaire for less than two weeks and had just started learning Swahili. I knew only how to greet people and say my name. While walking down this side road, I decided to practice my Swahili. A woman was walking toward me. She had a baby tied to her back and a heavy load balanced on her head. By her manner of dress, I knew that she was very poor. As she drew near, I said, "Jambo, mama" ("Hello, mother"), a traditional and formulaic greeting. In response, she raised her hands, crossed them over her heart, and replied, "Jambo, mutoto *wangu*" ("Hello, *my* child"). I could not believe that this poor African woman would call me—an upper-middle-class white Westerner—*her* child. I might have initiated this exchange, but she reached out and invited me into relationship with her. She was the missionary; I was the converted.

The person most influential in my conversion journey, however, was the Right Reverend Emmanuel Kolini, the bishop of the Diocese of Shaba. He was a powerful leader for all of us working in the diocese—Zairian and foreign alike. But to me, as a young American volunteer, Bishop Kolini reached out and helped me become aware—aware of different cultures, aware of the deep meaning of relationships between people in community, both in his culture and on a global scale.

I accompanied him one day to a worship service in another denomination's church at which he was the guest preacher. The service was longer than the Anglican services I had been to. It lasted for hours! The congregation sang and danced, and the bishop preached a powerful sermon. But it was hot. Mercifully, after the service, we were served soft drinks. I was offered an orange Fanta and accepted gratefully. I was so thirsty that I couldn't help but gulp it down. The man in charge of the drinks offered me another one. I thought, "It's pretty sugary, but why not? I'm still thirsty, and we'll be going home soon." So I drank another Fanta. My thirst was only partially quenched, and I was beginning to get a sugar headache when Bishop Kolini said we were going. "Good," I thought. "As soon as I get home I'll have a large glass of cold water." We got in the car and pulled away ... only to pull up to the chief pastor's house. I hoped that we were dropping him off, but it was not to be. We were all invited for lunch.

While waiting for lunch to appear we sat and drank . . . more Fanta! Our host reminded me of hosts at cocktail parties who fill people's wine glasses, whether the guests care for more or not. By the time we sat at the table I had drunk at least one more Fanta, and our host kept pouring. Finally, I looked over to Bishop Kolini and begged him (in English) to tell our host to stop. My bishop smiled, laughed, and said, "Ah, but this is African hospitality. You don't have a choice!"

African hospitality was much more "over the top" than what I was used to. What little this man had he spent in lavishing Fanta and food on us! But what I could not yet understand was that these actions built relationships, which were more important than money. Relationships kept the community together, saw people through difficult times, kept food on the table. Relationships were life itself. In that context, how dare I refuse more Fanta?

This host, the woman on the road, Bishop Kolini, and many other Africans confronted my life and broke open my worldview. They invited me to become aware. Their love, conversations, and challenges motivated me to see more clearly, to act more justly, and to ask forgiveness more readily when I fell short. Their liberating first words and deeds freed me to become a friend. They converted me, and *only then* was I able to be a part of others' conversions—to be a true friend. Through these relationships I came to a deeper understanding of the oneness we have in Christ, despite cultural, economic, and racial differences.

DEVELOPMENTS BACK HOME

I now switch gears to what might seem unrelated to my Zairian experience. While the circumstances and issues appeared different on the surface, the underlying themes were remarkably similar to those of my experience in Zaire. From 1993 to 1997, I was the assistant to the rector in a parish. The rector and I got along great and formed an incredible team, and the church was alive and thriving. Then, in November 1996, I fell in love with a woman. I was overjoyed with this new love in my life. I knew, however, that dating a woman in the same town as my parish was bound to cause gossip, so I decided to "come out" to my rector. Falling in love and coming out were the catalysts for yet another great conversion experience. At first (but not for long), I naïvely thought that life could carry on as usual. After all, my bishop here at home knew about my sexuality and just thanked me for sharing. He felt that my rector could handle it as well. Besides, my rector and I had shared much over the past three years.

About a week after coming out to my rector, we had a meeting. He was visibly uncomfortable. In my gut, I knew what was coming, and I thought,

"What happened to our great relationship?" He, like official church statements, told me that I had three choices as he saw it: (a) I could pursue a ministry opportunity I was looking into; (b) I could stay at my present parish; or
(c) I could date this woman. I wanted to stay at my present parish and to date
this woman, but that wasn't one of the choices. So without hesitation, I
"picked" (c). I tried to tell my boss that the choice wasn't about dating a
woman. It was about being able to look at myself in the mirror each day and
to know I was being true to who I was—who I thought God had created me
to be. I realize that this statement might be difficult for some who hold more
conservative views than I do. All I can say is that, through prayer, counsel,
and soul-searching, I believe that God created me as I am.

The long and the short is that, while we did try to work out a way for me
to stay, after a few months I was "encouraged to seek a new call." There was
no discussion with the vestry—let alone the parish—only a vague letter to
parishioners saying that the rector felt I should be encouraged to seek a new
call and that the parish should look at a change in its ministry staff. As in some
games, I hadn't just come up against a limit. I had set off an alarm that dis-
qualified me from playing further.

My experience of falling in love and coming out to my rector, like my time
in Zaire, confronted my life and broke open my worldview. It was beginning
to dawn on me that life could not go on as usual: not in this parish, not in
my ministry, not in my life. I was learning more about the nature of relationships—this time that they are fragile. I was learning what it felt like to be
an outsider, to be silenced, and especially to be made to feel that this was all
my fault. The unspoken message was that if I weren't there, everything would
be fine and back to normal. But given the current state of our church, my sexuality—whether I like it or not—was a community issue and should have
been dealt with *in* community. Instead, the way it was handled cut me off from
community. How different this was from my African experience, in which
community formed the context for dealing with all issues. How different this
was from Jesus, who invited all people, including tax collectors and Samari-
tans, to be in relationship. Jesus never wished that anyone would go away.

MUTUALLY EXCLUDING CATEGORIES?

When I tell my LGBT/queer[2] friends about my profoundly meaningful
missionary experience in Zaire, they give me quizzical looks. It's hard enough
for some of them to wrap their brains around the fact that I am queer and
Christian. Queer and missionary, however, is more than some can handle. On
the other hand, when I tell—if I tell—my missionary friends about my sexu-

ality, they, too, get a "does not compute" look. How do I hold these apparently mutually exclusive aspects of my life together?

My Generation X perspective helps me affirm that these two aspects of my life do not contradict but reinforce each other. More specifically, three GenX commitments implicit in my experiences in Africa and at home enable me to bridge these two identities: openness to the world, priority on relationship, and acceptance of provisionality.

Going to Africa shortly after graduating from college was a very GenX thing to do. Our generation has grown up in a time when phone, fax, and E-mail have enabled us to be in touch with people regardless of the miles between us. The news media (epitomized by CNN) bring information, events, and stories into our living rooms twenty-four hours a day, seven days a week. We not only read about what is happening on the other side of the world, we see live footage. Travel has become more commonplace and affordable. Depending on the season, it is cheaper for me to fly to London than Chicago. Economic markets are also more closely linked, with good and bad results. While I appreciate what globalization has brought us—my strawberries come from Mexico and my apples from New Zealand; my favorite shirt was made in China and my favorite shoes in Sri Lanka—it has also made it easier for the United States to exploit weaker neighbors around the world.

For Xers, this exposure has created a generation open to different languages, cultures, tastes, and beliefs. Generation X is more aware that much of what we hold sacred—whether certain religious beliefs or most political opinions—is conditioned by our contexts: where and how we grew up.[3] This means that two people, growing up in different contexts, could have different but equally valid beliefs. This is not to say that all beliefs are equal. But because a particular belief is not an explicit part of the Christian tradition does not mean that it is automatically inferior or wrong. *Different* no longer necessarily means "wrong" or "bad." Exposure to difference actually helps us understand ourselves better while appreciating others.

Another GenX commitment is priority on relationships. Someone (a Baby Boomer) said to me recently, "You know, it was during my generation that we started to lose a sense of community. But your generation grew up in the midst of that loss." This is one reason my generation values strong relationships: we know how rare they are. When I was little, I knew only two kids whose parents were divorced. That changed dramatically by college. Now a large percentage of people live in single-parent or "blended" families.

As a nation, we are also extremely mobile. In my family, at one point I lived in Zaire, my brother Bruce in Denmark, my two oldest brothers in southern California, and my parents in Illinois. My mother was thrilled when we were all in the United States, even though we still stretched from coast to coast. With all this moving, it is hard to develop and keep strong relationships. This makes it more difficult for our roots to grow.

My time in Africa taught me about the importance—no, the absolute necessity—of good relationships and community. Living in a culture that valued people over things was beautiful. My African bishop once commented, "I don't know if I could live in the U.S. You have homeless people and so many isolated people. People over there are depressed and some even kill themselves. Here, we might be poor, but no one is alone."

Many African sayings reinforce the importance of community. In Kenya they say, "I am because we are." In South Africa they say, "A person is a person because of other persons." How different these sayings are from the Western expression, "I think, therefore I am." In Africa, I experienced something I didn't know was missing in my life: lives lived in deep community. Because of this fact, people could not always act as they pleased. When there was a problem, it was worked out in community. Ideally, conversion occurred on both sides, rather than one side winning all and the other losing all. Walking away or ending the relationship was not an option.

Strong emphasis on community can also have negative aspects. Too much group identity can squelch a person's unique self. When this happens, however, the group is no longer a community, but a cult. True community affirms the importance of everyone while also encouraging each to be what God calls each to be. True community helps us know who we are, as a group and as individuals. Staunch individualism, which is too common in the United States, reduces our ability to know who we are because it isolates us from the community. We cannot know ourselves apart from community.

The experience of coming out to my former rector also underscored the importance of relationships. Before coming out to him, our relationship was strong and mutually supportive. We each grew from this relationship— sometimes comforting, sometimes confronting. After coming out and the difficult last months, I realized that relationships are also fragile. Sometimes they grow and deepen with change, sometimes they do not—not that I would have stayed in the closet to keep my job or my relationship with the rector. But I now know the difficulty of balancing the importance of one relationship with new understandings of others.

Lastly, Generation X accepts provisionality. By this statement I do not mean that we have no means of arriving at truth, but that truth is always becoming. Sometimes new evidence and insights show that deeply held beliefs and opinions are false. For example, centuries ago people believed that the sun revolved around the earth. When Galileo proved otherwise, the church forced him to retract this truth. It was centuries before the church accepted that Galileo was right. Sometimes, however, new evidence and insights affirm more deeply what we already believe to be true. New archaeological finds help us understand aspects of evolution more fully.

As an Xer, my life has spanned more technological breakthroughs than all previous generations. And with this technology comes change—constant change. One young person commented,

> For my great-grandparents, change was slow. They invented the car. For my grandparents, change was a little faster. They invented the television. For my parents, change has been rapid. They invented the computer. But for my generation, change is constant. We don't have time to think about it.[4]

Take a classic example: when I was in the market to buy a computer a few years ago, I asked a friend for help. Pointing to a computer in a catalog, I asked, "Is this the computer I should buy?" She answered, "Yes, unless you can wait a few months. If you can wait, they'll be coming out with a new model that is faster and has more power at the same price." Something new and radical is discovered every day. We learn about the existence of galaxies as well as the discovery of subatomic particles. The experience is amazing and dizzying at the same time as discoveries make accepted theories obsolete. New discoveries also create a new set of questions. This isn't always easy. But that is life at the end of the second millennium.

IMPLICATIONS FOR THE CHURCH

God's mission, in which the church participates, is "to restore all people to unity with God and each other in Christ."[5] Openness to the world, priority on relationships, and acceptance of provisionality—all GenX commitments—can help the church revitalize its participation in this mission. I discovered these three commitments on the margins of the world—first as a missionary in Zaire and then as an out queer person here at home. These three commitments can help us, as a church, live together and participate in God's one mission of restoration and reconciliation.

If we, as a church, listen to one another long enough, we may not agree, but will come to understand better the basis for our differing positions. Personally, I have found this easier to do with people from other parts of the world than with my brothers and sisters in Christ at home. I think this is because I assume people at home are like me and should, therefore, believe as I do. I know people from Zaire or China are different, so I don't expect to see eye-to-eye on all issues. In fact, I look to them to learn new things. Maybe we can begin to allow for difference within our own church and view it not as a problem but as an asset. Paul wrote that there is one body with many parts. Each part, although different from the rest, is indispensable (1 Cor. 12:12–27).

This leads to another point: whether we like each other or not, we need each other. As the eye cannot say to the ear, "Because you are not an eye, I don't need you," neither can the bishop of Newark say to the bishop of Quincy, Ilinois, "Because you do not believe in women's ordination, I don't need you." Nor can I say to someone who does not affirm LGBT/queer relationships, "Because you don't affirm this, I don't need you." We are all parts of the body of Christ. In fact, it is not even our choice. Jesus said, "You did not choose me but I chose you" (John 15:16). We are in relationship because Jesus has first chosen to be in relationship with each of us. Can we commit to finding ways to live together—to be a viable and authentic community of faith that can disagree and debate, even passionately, but without demonizing the other or without threatening schism? What about the promises we reaffirm every time we say our baptismal covenant: to respect the dignity of every human being—not just those on the opposite side of the world but those on the opposite side of an issue as well? Do we value each other and our relationships enough?

Lastly, can we acknowledge, as Paul writes, that "we know only in part" and that "now we see in a mirror, dimly" (1 Cor. 13:9, 12)? Can we admit, with the same humility as Paul's admission, that our beliefs and doctrine are at best provisional? God's perspective may not change, but ours is always deepening and changing when necessary. Can we acknowledge that this has always been so in the church—that we have changed our minds on many positions previously held dear, like Gentile inclusion, equality for people of color, women's leadership roles, just to name a few? As Mark Harris writes, this experience of provisionality is "the sense that all that we have as doctrine is provisionally stated, and awaits the full disclosure of God for completion."[6] Again, this does not mean that "anything goes."

How do we assess, then, "what goes"? Our standard is holy scripture as understood through the lenses of reason, tradition, and experience. Jesus said that you will know a tree by its fruits. A good tree cannot bear bad fruit. Neither can a bad tree bear good fruit (Matt. 7:16–18). We are all called to keep striving after truth, knowing that this is a lifelong call. Paul wrote, "Not that I have already obtained this or have already reached the goal; but I press on to make it my own, because Christ Jesus has made me his own. . . . This one thing I do: forgetting what lies behind me and straining forward to what lies ahead, I press on toward the goal for the prize of the heavenly call of God in Christ Jesus" (Phil. 3:12–14). We are called to keep pressing on, discerning God's truth in community, knowing that we do not yet "fully know." I can hold on to my convictions and beliefs while remaining open to how others perceive the same issues. Perhaps God does not want to convert others through me. Perhaps God wishes to convert me through others.

I firmly believe that the church should welcome all people, including LGBT/queer people, and that it should bless our unions and ordain our people—"practicing" or not. I do not believe that this position is incompatible with scripture or tradition or reason. I want and expect the church to move in this direction, but I am also willing to stay in relationship with those who disagree with me, and I am willing to be in dialogue with them. Dialogue means continuing to talk with and to listen to those who differ from me. It means getting to know others and trying to understand why they believe what they do. It means trying to find common ground and putting our differences in the context of a community of ever deepening relationships in Christ's love. Contrary to popular opinion, shared beliefs are not the foundation of a relationship—love is. Shared beliefs might help contribute to that relationship, but so, too, might differing beliefs.

Unity does not depend on uniformity. Difference, as in the body, is crucial. Dialogue means valuing the relationships we have and remembering that they are fragile. Dialogue also means speaking the truth in love. Dialogue means never feeling justified in saying, "Because you don't hold my position, I don't need you." Nor is it justifiable to say, "Because I don't agree with their views, I guess they don't need me." We all need each other. Schism is a scandal in our already divided world. Jesus prayed that we might be one as he and the Father are one (John 17:20–23). Dialogue means striving for oneness without compromising our integrity.

Recently, Gathering the NeXt Generation was trying to come up with a slogan for a banner at General Convention 2000. One phrase that seemed to have the approval of many was, "Clergy transcending issues through relationships." These clergy represent the spectrum of religious thought. Some oppose the ordination of women and of LGBT/queer people. Others affirm the ordination of women and of LGBT/queer people. But all of us recognize that we are in the community of Christ, and we like it that way. I don't know if and when certain issues will be transcended, but I do know the issues that currently divide us can only be dealt with through genuine, loving relationships.[7]

This is, after all, what mission is about: restoring to unity that which is broken or divided. What better way to be in mission than to start the restoration and reconciliation process with ourselves? What a witness that would be for others. No doctrine will accomplish this task—only love. To paraphrase Paul, "If I have all wisdom and know all the right answers to life's moral dilemmas, and yet do not have love, I am nothing, and I gain nothing" (1 Cor. 13:1–3). Only love can restore us to unity. Jesus commanded us to put priority on relationships by commanding us to love one another (John 13:34; 15:13; 15:17).

My bishop from Africa was one of the bishops at the 1998 Lambeth Conference who voted against affirming homosexuals, blessing their relationships, or ordaining them if "practicing." On top of that, since Lambeth this bishop has been at the forefront of pressuring the Episcopal Church in the United States to conform to this view. While conventional wisdom would say that the two of us could not continue to be true friends, in reality we have stayed very close. We challenge each other's beliefs; we affirm each other where we see God working in our lives; we pray for each other; and we continue to love each other. We are able to stay in relationship because we respect each other, know that God is at work in and through us, and know that our understanding of any issue is not complete. Lastly, we trust that God is working God's purpose in us, in the church, and in the world. This allows each of us to hold onto our dearly held beliefs a little more loosely.

Generation X's openness to the world and its ways, our priority on relationships, and our acceptance of provisionality are three commitments that can be of great use to the church at this time. Our generation can help the church find ways to live together and to move through current debates. We have much to offer the church. My only question is whether or not the church will hear our voices and value our perspectives.

NOTES

1. Zaire has since been renamed the Democratic Republic of the Congo, and the Anglican Diocese of Shaba is now called the Anglican Diocese of Katanga.
2. "LGBT" refers to "lesbian, gay, bisexual, and transgendered." People within the LGBT/queer community refer to themselves in any number of ways. This is why I use the acronym as well as "queer."
3. In fact, the incarnation of Christ can be understood as God in context.
4. Greg, 19, of Newberg, Oregon, quoted in Craig Kenneth Miller, *Postmoderns: The Beliefs, Hopes, and Fears of Young Americans (1965–1981)* (Nashville: Discipleship Resources, 1996), 17.
5. *BCP* 855.

6. Mark Harris, *The Challenge of Change: The Anglican Communion in the Post-modern Era* (New York: Church Publishing, 1998), 79.
7. For more ideas on how to have meaningful conversations about sexuality with a group from all sides of the religious and sexual spectrum, see the Web site www.bridges-across.org. This Web site and organization of the same name are dedicated to building bridges on all sides of the sexuality issue.

PREPARING FOR LUKE:

Reflections by a Pregnant Priest

Kate Moorehead

I found out that I was pregnant in early December, just as I began to prepare for my first Christmas at St. John's Church. As the church began to prepare for the arrival of the incarnation, I was beginning to prepare for the arrival of a new life. Part of me couldn't believe it was happening. For weeks, I went about my business as usual. Perhaps I was afraid of becoming too attached to the tiny, fragile life inside me. Other issues loomed on the horizon. As a young pregnant priest, I had no role models. My husband and I were thrilled, but confounded. How exactly does one break this kind of news?

How do you tell your congregation that the assistant rector they hired just six months ago will be taking a maternity leave in eight more months? When do you inform the rector? How do you let the rest of the parish know? A newsletter? The good old grapevine method (which, no doubt, would work quickly)?

Certainly, the church as a whole has no traditions regarding pregnant priests. Before 1976, no such person existed. When women were first ordained, most of them already had given birth to their children; many were empty nesters.[1] So while Boomer and "silent"-generation women were the trailblazers, the full implications of this historic development in the priesthood have yet to be played out fully. Generation X is the first generation to face fully the impact of childbearing on the priestly vocation. Women priests of my generation face a new set of questions and decisions—some of them purely practical and others deeply theological.

Our first decision seemed clear. God called my husband and me to wait. Many women still feel it is better to announce pregnancy after three months have passed and the pregnancy is relatively secure. Who would want to take a parish on that roller-coaster ride? So my husband and I enjoyed our news privately for a while and, in retrospect, this was good for our marriage. We smiled at one another often: at home, in church. God had given us a gift, and we savored the moment before making it public. To share something so exciting, so profound, naturally drew us closer to one another. By the time we spread the news, we had digested it and were ready to share it with others.

Somehow I managed to get through New Year's Eve without drinking champagne, and no one seemed to notice.

I was ordained to the priesthood in early February, just as my third month of pregnancy rolled around. I decided to tell Joe, the rector of St. John's, before the ordination, since he had some summer schedule changes to make. The rest of the parish could be informed after I was ordained to the priesthood. Luckily it was winter, so no one at my ordination service noticed that my largest skirt could not be buttoned in the back.

Was the child ordained? A few of my peers in the ordinands' training program joked about this. One parishioner asked it seriously. My answer was no, of course not. Apostolic succession, in my understanding, is no magic trick. If an acolyte tried to get too close to the event and his robe touched mine, he certainly would not be ordained. In the same way, this child had come to share my body, but had by no means consented to this whole thing. Without consent, simply touching me was not enough, in my mind, to call the child ordained. I do realize, however, that my view requires an understanding of apostolic succession as dependent on more than the physical phenomenon of laying on of hands. I believe that one must agree to, desire, and be devoted to the gospel in order for the ordination to be valid. So, no, I told my parishioner, the child was not ordained.

It was, however, a joy to share the ordination service with that tiny one inside me. The presence of that life was in the back of my mind during the entire service. Did s/he feel the surge of joy and awe I felt? Did the child somehow absorb the beauty of the event? Did s/he hear the hymns reverberate inside me? I'm glad that the baby was part of it all and shared it with me.

Joe was kind when I broke the news. Actually he guessed that I was pregnant before I told him. "I have news," I said. "You're pregnant," he responded. It made me wonder if I had done something to give it away.

Joe's usual habit of escaping abroad in August was shattered. His new young assistant, finally ordained a priest and able to take on services by herself, would be going on maternity leave. The baby was due in early August. Although I had asked about maternity leave when I applied for the job, I don't think he expected such a speedy delivery. But kindness prevailed over shock. I asked for a six-week maternity leave as per diocesan guidelines; he offered me twelve weeks paid.

Now for the rest of the parish. My husband and I decided to let the news spread itself. No other method of informing people felt right. How strange it would be to mail a letter just to tell folks I was pregnant—a parishwide birth announcement. An article in the parish newsletter was out. I even pictured getting up at announcements on Sunday, "Oh, and by the way, I am with child." No. Although the parish needed to know, it wasn't formal parish business. It was *my* child!

I was the first permanent woman priest on staff at St. John's. Before taking the job, I wondered about maternity leave. Because Generation X is the first generation to have women clergy as an accepted norm, many dioceses did not have written policies about maternity leave.[2] Luckily, the Diocese of Connecticut did have a maternity-leave clause in its diocesan guidelines, so I had it written into my contract. Thus, when I approached the vestry, things went smoothly. Maybe they had been forewarned, but they approved the twelve weeks recommended by the rector.

As time went on, of course, my belly began to bulge. Chasubles hid a lot, but questions still arose: Could I celebrate adequately? Did I get tired standing up? What about consuming the wine? (Someone else would have to do it.) People seemed concerned, but kind. Not one nasty comment was made. People seemed generally worried about me. Was I going to be OK? Would I be able to function as their priest? They seemed to follow my lead, however. If I appeared comfortable with the whole thing, they were comforted.

Still, their anxiety led me to wonder whether my effectiveness as a priest was somehow hampered by my pregnancy—a question none of my male colleagues and few of my Boomer and silent-generation women colleagues had ever had to face. The largest concern had to do with returning to work. As the pregnancy progressed, many parishioners, especially women, did not believe that I would come back. There seemed to be an unspoken assumption that once I held my child in my arms, I would quit my job and vow to stay at home for at least five years. Women who had diligently remained at home with their children assumed I would also be a "good" mother and stay at home. If I didn't stay at home, could I be a good mother? And if I wasn't a good mother to my child, could I be a good priest to them? They felt conflicted. They wanted to believe that I would be a good mother to my child, and yet they didn't want to lose me as their priest. They were forced to acknowledge my human needs while continuing to rely on me as their priest. This was a new, difficult position for the parish, and they looked to me for guidance. If being a mother and a priest was an impossible scenario, they trusted that I would let them know.

To jump ahead in my story, the decision to return to work was not an easy one. Part of me still feels that perhaps good mothers do stay at home, but to sacrifice my passion, my vocation, for my child might have caused me to resent that child, and that would be far worse than working. No, God would have me—love would have me—be both a priest and a mother. As I returned to work after the birth—slowly, quietly—the women of the parish watched me manage my life. The criticism was never overt, and gradually it has faded. Now they seem to chalk up my decision to a new era, a new era and a good husband.

The church has a long way to go before it fully integrates the societal changes that have accompanied the rejection of many traditional gender roles. As a member of Generation X, I have always pictured my Boomer elders as the trailblazers. As I understand it, part of the Boomer complaint against GenX "slackers" is that the Boomers did all the work while GenX reaps all the benefits. But I think it's important for us all to realize that what the Boomers began is not yet complete, especially in the church. It will largely be up to my generation to build upon, revise, and struggle with the work begun by earlier generations.

◄○►

And so my belly grew and grew. There was no denying that I was pregnant. The congregation, for the most part, developed along with me. It made me realize why God made pregnancy last so long. We all had nine months to get ourselves ready for the event. The baby showers were fast and furious. I started a group for young mothers, which I loved. I savored our meetings each month, when I listened to women discuss nursing and bottles, diapers, storytelling, discipline, and keeping the house clean. We talked about how to teach our children about God. As I listened to my parishioners talk about parenting, I pictured myself in the same role. With each day, I grew more excited. The mothers' group seemed to embrace me as a naïve, nervous new mom who also happened to be their priest. My vulnerability allowed them to share their own crises and fears, and from that I learned a great deal about becoming not only a better parent but a better priest as well. A number of young women mothers joined the church as a result of their participation in the group; they felt welcomed and honored as mothers. They didn't seem to mind teaching their priest about child rearing.

As one can imagine, I received many gifts. "Is this OK?" I asked Joe. "Sure, enjoy it," he said. The parish literally showered me. I felt very loved. People knit and sewed, shopped and baked. I felt guilty at times. Would I be receiving this many gifts if I were not their priest? Probably not, but we did enjoy ourselves. The parish seemed energized. I was busy writing thank-you notes, telling each person how much their gift meant to me. This helped relieve my guilt, but it also gave me a chance to write to each parishioner individually. In anticipating and celebrating the arrival of a new life we grew closer as a parish family. As one cleans a house before receiving a guest, we primped and prepared for a new baby. Everyone was helping me get ready, but they were getting ready too. Perhaps, in some small way, this birth helped us to be hospitable to our Lord, to prepare for the day of his coming, whenever that day may come.

My pregnancy also provided the opportunity for women parishioners to tell their own stories. Labor pain, swelled feet, birth defects, and miscarriages all came up in conversation. Slowly, the stories came out of the woodwork. Not in a formal office setting, but in hallways, the sacristy, and other places where we found ourselves alone. I struggled to be pastoral with people whose stories frightened me. Children were born dead. Labor prolonged. Doctors made mistakes. I saw a new side of the parish in the women who held these stories inside. One woman opened up to me: "My child died and the doctor didn't even stay by my side. . . ." The silence of a stillborn, almost too painful to mention after all these years. I remember swallowing hard.

"I'm so sorry," I said.

"I don't mean to scare you."

"No, its OK."

I was honored by their confidences, and overwhelmed at the same time. I was also afraid. I wanted to run from some stories as if they might be contagious, as if just listening might affect the life and health of the child I carried. Inside, priest and mother wrestled against each other, each trying to listen with understanding.

Women also came with advice. At times, I felt more like a daughter than a priest. Eat this, exercise in this way . . . drink, drink, drink . . . and everyone always wanted to know how I was feeling. My body was a regular topic of conversation. For the most part, I found this nurturing. But at times I wondered whether they would feel free to come to me, to rely on me as their priest when they were consumed with taking care of me. I suppose this is a dilemma all Generation X priests encounter in their ministry: How do we minister to those who are older and have more life experience? I couldn't hide the process I was going through, so I just decided to be myself. If they chose not to burden me with their pastoral issues at that time, well, it wasn't because I couldn't handle it. My belly might have been large, but my hearing was just fine. I was still with them, there was just more of me.

My pregnancy was a very healthy one, thanks be to God. I felt great, with energy and vigor. I ate like a horse and was constantly excusing myself to go to the bathroom. Would the sacred order of priests be demeaned by my hourly trips to the latrine? It didn't seem so.

Early on, I asked my husband, "What about a *doula* or midwife?" "Are you crazy?" he said. "I don't want some hippie delivering our child!" But, in his usual fashion, J. D. listened despite his loud reaction. A few weeks later, he was buying camping gear at a yard sale when he met Cynthia, a midwife, and they started talking. "Birth is a sacred experience," she said. He was sold. I was too. I then realized that the experience of having a child was a deeply religious one for us all.

The months passed. At the beginning of Lent, Joe, the rector, scheduled a vacation for July, my ninth month. A few of my colleagues marveled that he would leave me alone with the entire parish. I felt honored. I did not want to be coddled. Certainly he deserved a break, given that he would be on his own for three months. And he was smart enough not to go abroad, but to vacation at home in case of an early arrival.

I sat through Good Friday and could not help but wonder how Mary survived seeing her child murdered. That child had come out of her. Didn't she still sometimes recall how he had moved deep within her? How his personality and his tranquillity were known to her even then? How did she do it? I sat in silence for three hours on Good Friday, feeling my child move inside my belly. Although I couldn't kneel that day, my heart knelt as it had never knelt before.

By the grace of God, someone donated an air-conditioning system that was installed in the nave in the late spring. Without it, I might not have been able to stand for three services in the heat. I warned Joe, that, if I had to, I would not wear the chasuble. A light alb and stole would have to suffice. That extra layer was just too hot. Toward the end of July, I almost took a chair to the narthex to greet people as they left the service, but it never came to that.

In my ninth month, I performed a baptism for the child of a woman in the mothers' group. It was particularly poignant for me to maneuver that child around my belly. As I poured the water over the child's head, I thought of the waters inside my own body, where a child was bathed in safety and innocence. No wonder we return to water to cleanse ourselves in a spiritual new birth. I knew whose child would probably be baptized next.

My labor began early on a Saturday morning. I was in labor for twenty-two hours. One parishioner had asked me to notify her when I went into labor, so that a prayer chain could be activated—but I was hesitant. This miraculous event, which was about to happen, was so private. I did not call that woman, but the parish found out anyway. The prayer chain, which had not been my idea, was activated. Unfortunately a few were left out of the loop, and feelings were hurt. But I knew they were out there, caring and praying for us, and that helped.

Luke Taylor Moorehead, nine pounds, five ounces, was born on a Sunday morning, August 9, at 1:35 A.M. Parishioners came to church that morning, and evidently the ushers told them, "It's a boy!" as soon as each person entered the building. The birth was also celebrated with a loud cheer during the announcement time. Somebody wanted to hang a sign outside the church door: "It's a boy!" I was relieved that no one followed up on that plan. Maybe at Christmastime that sign would have been appropriate.

Other than the rector, who blessed Luke, and our deacon, no one visited us in the hospital, per my request. It was our time, my time with my husband and our new little one.

My maternity leave, although it was exactly what I needed, was a delicate time for my relationship with the parish. For months prior to Luke's birth, I had debated whether I should attend St. John's with the baby. My decision was no. Luke would be tiny, and it would not be good for him to be surrounded by well-wishers. I also knew that to attend St. John's would be to return to work. Much as I considered this my parish home, it was also my place of employment. Again, the balance between priest and mother was a difficult one, but the parish seemed to understand my decision. When asked if I would attend St. John's, I explained that if I came to church I'd be inclined to work and that I needed time to rest. There was also an unspoken understanding that it was not healthy to take a little baby in public before the child was a few months old. Both the parishioners and I were learning as we went along.

Parishioners did visit us at home, and they brought food! Dinners for mother and dad, who had stayed up all night and had to eat, were like treasure. Home-cooked meals. For the most part, the visits to my home were wonderful. People knew the chaos of having a very young child, and generally they did not stay long. Luke was also a remarkably good baby, so I could be flexible with people and visit. Women came, and we talked as I nursed. Some of the visits were pastoral, in that a person came to confide in me about something in her life, but most were just friendly chats. The men tended to come only with their wives in the evening, and I was comfortable with that. For the most part, the visits curbed my loneliness during the months when I was alone with the baby.

All this is to say that it can be done: pregnant priests do exist, and it does work. Pregnancy focuses the priest and congregation on many of the issues that already exist in the priesthood, particularly for young clergy. For instance, how is a priest supposed to experience life's milestones for the first time and simultaneously to guide a congregation in its faith development? Does one have to have life experience to pastor a congregation? Can one be in the midst of life's greatest changes while ministering to others? Can one's life itself be made incarnate in such a way as to model the life of faith? I believe that congregations are hungry for priests who are open about their humanity, and that includes areas that priests have not yet experienced. The greatest forms of ministry can take place when the pastor allows him or herself to be pastored. An honest priest, who tries to live through life's milestones openly, allows parishioners to admit their own lack of experience, struggles, and pain. Because I have had a child, people seem to confide in me even more. As long as boundaries are maintained, inexperience can be a blessing for both priest and parish.

That this inexperience can be a blessing for both priest and parish was probably one of the most profound insights I gained from my pregnancy. In the ordination process and throughout the church, inexperience is often viewed as a liability. To an extent, the church has bought into the corporate mind-set that a person's qualifications must include a minimum of experience, a minimum that, in most cases, is determined arbitrarily. But my pregnancy taught me that inexperience can be an asset in ministry. Jesus' own actions in calling inexperienced disciples bears witness to this paradoxical truth. Perhaps one of the greatest gifts that Generation X can give the church is the gift of grace-filled inexperience. Like the disciples, we will stumble and fail to understand. But I also hope that, like the disciples, we will help the church grow into a community of discipleship that will "turn the world upside down" (Acts 17:6).

It was crucial not to try to hold myself out as wise beyond my years or to pretend that I was not afraid. Rather, I tried to be open, to share my fear, amazement, and wonder at the child developing inside me. I wanted to speak honestly and to give others permission to speak honestly about their lives. Birth was not a taboo subject. I tried to be open about the fact that my pregnancy brought me closer to God. Through this experience, I realized that I was free to be open and to share my fear, amazement, and wonder about other aspects of my life and ministry. It was freeing.

To be sure, I felt insecure at times. What kind of a priest admits to being frightened of labor pains? I worried that parishioners would be consumed with reassuring me and that I would not be considered a resource in their own times of transition. The pastoral aspect of my ministry concerned me most. But as long as I did not depend on parishioners for moral support, but was open about my inexperience, the relationship of trust remained. I have never looked to my parishioners for counseling or moral guidance, but I have been honest with them about my struggles. There is a fine line in the ministry between sharing oneself and emotional dependency.

Sharing one's personal life with a parish is both a blessing and a curse. It seems that I am always struggling to achieve a balance between honesty, which promotes openness and trust in the community, and maintaining boundaries, so that my personal life remains my own. I believe this is a judgment call for all ages in the priesthood, and part of the tension in which we serve—the tension between the human being and the sacred order.

The paradigm for the Episcopal priesthood is changing. The idea that priests are one step removed from the parish, starched straight in shirt and collar, is falling by the wayside. Parishioners are increasingly hungry for human priests who admit their shortcomings, who admit that life can be a struggle. It is vital that we live into this new model of the priesthood. Generation X is described as skeptical of authority. In order to reach this generation, a priest must admit to the struggle that is part of life. Generation X wants to share a relationship with their priests that is both human and substantive. We need the gospel to be enfleshed not just in the sacrament but also in the life of the one who officiates the sacrament. We must admit our frailties and dependence on God. GenX priests, pregnant or not, often share these characteristics with the generation as a whole and are thus able to minister in this changing context.

Pregnancy forced me to integrate my human frailties into my ministry. There was no avoiding my physical needs, no avoiding my sexuality or health. I was a person, just like all other people of the parish, and parishioners saw aspects of their own experiences reflected in my nine-month journey. The result has been the opening of many new lines of communication.

I write this reflection not to tell other GenX priests how to cope with pregnancy but to share my struggles and to convey that pregnancy is not a time-out from priesthood. Pregnancy can enhance one's ministry. Pregnancy is a journey that the entire parish undertakes. It is a journey filled with expectation, joy, confusion, and newness. All relationships are called into question as we await the arrival of another person into the world and into our circle of intimacy. If a priest is open and honest, the journey of pregnancy can bring both priest and parish to a deeper understanding of the miracle of birth, the gift of personhood, and the mystery of faith. Just as I was forever changed by becoming a mother, so the parish was changed. Together, we discovered one of the greatest gifts that God has given, the gift of life.

NOTES

1. Older women clergy entered the priesthood in large numbers in the early 1980s. Paula Nesbitt writes that these women were believed to be "house-

wives whose children are gone, divorcees, or women who've been work-
ing around the church so long they think they might as well run it"
("Feminization of American Clergy: Occupational Life Changes in the
Ordained Ministry" [Ph.D. diss., Harvard University, 1990], 206).

2. How many dioceses have written maternity-leave policies? After numerous phone calls, the Episcopal Church Center at 815 Second Avenue was
unable to answer my question. I was directed to the Church Pension Fund.
The Pension Fund also has no record of maternity-leave policies for clergy.

SECTION
FOUR

MISSION
AND MINISTRY
FOR THE
NEW MILLENNIUM

THE FUTURE OF
OUR GENERATION
IN THE CHURCH

J. Scott Barker

I graduated from Berkeley Divinity School at Yale in May 1992. After saying goodbye to seminary friends, my spouse and I packed ourselves, one-year-old daughter, and two cats into a puny Toyota Starlet and headed halfway across America to Trinity Cathedral in Omaha, Nebraska. For six years I served as assistant to the cathedral dean and, more recently, have served also as vicar of a small, biracial mission church in an older, transitional Omaha neighborhood. The stories that follow illustrate concerns I have about my future—and the future of my brother and sister priests—as part of the coming generation of priest-leaders in the Episcopal Church.

THE QUESTION OF BALANCE

First and foremost, I confess that I have struggled since day one to achieve workable balance between my roles as husband and father, priest and pastor. I have frequently told a few people that I fear I am an inattentive and absent family man because I am a priest—and an unavailable and weary priest because I am a husband and parent.

Parishioners are still astonished—and sometimes offended—when I decline invitations to wedding rehearsal dinners and receptions. But I have all but given up attending these events. I cannot figure another way—especially in the spring and fall—to create meaningful family time when both my spouse and I work long weekday hours. I weasel out of many church-related activities that seem similarly "optional," in an effort to create time and energy for my spouse and kids.

It is not only church members who find me an elusive target. My family gets cheated, too. Although I err on the side of being physically present for

133

my family when possible, my best efforts to "be there" often fail miserably. Parish emergencies either cut into designated family time, or, more often, my own preoccupation with what's going on at church keeps me from being mentally and emotionally present to my wife and kids. (Poignant irony: as I typed the last sentence, my seven-year-old daughter called from school. "Why aren't you here, Daddy?" I had forgotten that this was my day to pick her up!)

I think that clergy in my generation experience this conflict in a different and more difficult way than our predecessors. The "priestly identity" is changing fast. The expectations of the church, American culture, and Episcopal priests themselves are all in flux. Nothing is what it was thirty years ago.

Today's Episcopal priests have spouses with careers of their own. For the first time, the demands of the priest's job do not automatically trump other demands in the family economy. But the people we serve—and the institutional church—don't always seem to understand that. I have been wounded in a sometimes raging crossfire, caught between the expectations of a congregation I love and the professional hopes and dreams of a loving partner.

Today's priests are not only expected to be superior pastors but superior spouses and parents as well. That's new, too. The priests I idolized as a child were giants in the church. But I have come to discover that many were terrible marriage partners and parents. GenX priests have few healthy models to teach us how to balance the difficult, and often competing, vocations of marriage and ministry. I for one am willing to fight to ensure that I do not fail in either the sacramental commitment of marriage or of holy orders, but I confess that some days it is a real struggle.

There are some good sources of help. Talking to peers has been a godsend—and not only priests but any woman or man who thinks about his or her job as a ministry, and who also struggles to be a good partner and parent. It also helps enormously to have a supportive rector and bishop. Mine are helpful—but their frequent admonitions to "go be with your family" would mean even more if I saw them doing the same!

Finally, my spouse and I have, at a couple of points in our ten years of marriage, used the help of a good marriage counselor. I have no doubt that those visits not only enriched our common life by modeling a willingness to get help, but also gave others the courage to seek assistance when needed.

I am concerned with the ability of our young priests to maintain a healthy balance between family life and professional life. Both our vocations and our relationships hang in the balance. I believe that this new generation of Episcopal clergy will either find new and creative ways to integrate and juggle our different roles as priests, pastors, spouses, and parents—or we will have more failed vocations and marriages than any previous generation of clergy.

THE EUCHARISTIC CENTER

Soon after my ordination to the priesthood, I was assigned to the rota of priests and bishops who said noonday Mass at Trinity Cathedral. At first, the excitement and privilege of helping to lead that worship was almost unbelievable. I would head to the cathedral's modest chapel thirty minutes early to mark the propers for the day, to make the altar look beautiful, and to say my own prayers of preparation in the silent splendor of the cathedral's Nativity Chapel.

But it did not take long for the novelty to wear off. Within a few months I became angry at the time I felt was "wasted" in saying that Mass. On a good day, maybe four people showed up. Not infrequently, no one would appear and, after saying the pro-anaphora to an empty chapel, I'd pack up and leave without even receiving the sacrament.

Especially vexing was that, although nobody was showing up to receive God's "spiritual gifts," scads were appearing at the front door for God's more tangible gifts: sack lunches, bus tokens, counseling, and prayer from a willing caregiver. By the time I'd been a priest for six months, I resented saying Mass on weekdays, because I thought there was more important work to do for God's people at the cathedral's doorstep.

Six years later, I am whistling a different tune, having regained appreciation for my noonday duties. The church's ministry is truly unique. The church prays corporately for humankind, and after nearly seven years of priestly ministry I now know what a difference those prayers make. Only the church promises—and provides—the real presence of the nourishing, healing, and liberating power of God's Son to a hungry, hurting, and captive people. There is no end to the human need that presents itself at the church door every day. After spending many hours at the county jail, courtrooms, and soup kitchens, my eyes have been opened.

As in my personal life, I seek balance between the altar and public ministry. I will continue to distribute sack lunches, to pay security deposits, to visit prisoners, and to be a pest on the opinion page of the local paper. But when the altar calls, I go in peace, secure that there are dedicated people committed to feeding the hungry, housing the homeless, and ministering to the physical and psychological hurts that an impoverished existence inflicts on our Lord in the person of the poor and outcast. I go to God's altar secure that these psychologists, counselors, and social workers are ministers as I am, and are as good (and better!) at meeting the needs than I am or will ever be.

I, like most clergy in my generation, am committed to social justice issues. But while I have no doubt that I do God's work when scooping soup at the local shelter, I believe that I make an even greater difference in a hungry world when I stand at the altar and celebrate the holy mysteries of the word become flesh. This is the greatest act I can do as a priest in the church.

This work is the eucharistic center of the priestly vocation—the great spiritual gift that priests offer. I am concerned that my generation of "social gospel"–minded peers will fail to keep this discipline at the heart of our ministries and will fail to keep it fresh. I believe that this generation of young clergy will either unapologetically provide these spiritual gifts to a broken world, or we will cease to matter as priests or as the body of Christ.

MEASURING SUCCESS

A couple of years ago, I was allowed to observe the work of a search committee looking for a new cathedral dean. It was an eye-opening experience. I'll never forget the meeting at which the group, by closely reviewing the candidates' résumés, cut the pool of applicants to a half-dozen. At one point, the facilitator characterized the résumé of a priest who had worked in several smaller start-up and mission ministries by saying, "This is the only person I've ever come across who's working her way *down* the ladder of success."

There is no "ladder of success" in ministry! Priests go where God calls us, and we do what needs to be done. We owe it to the church—and to our brothers and sisters in corporate America—to proclaim vigorously that a Christian's measure of success is not the biggest paycheck, the best benefit package or health care plan, but rather our willing submission to the mind of Christ.

Yet for me—and I dare say for all of us—submission to the mind of Christ is no easy task. My college and seminary education have ensured that I measure myself against classmates and friends who are in different stratospheres of earning potential and job mobility, and, as I get older, that gap widens. Some days I wonder whether Jesus wants a bright guy like me working for such modest compensation.

Moreover, I rarely have fun at work. The box that defines what a priest is "supposed" to do can be a tight fit. Between cranking out sermons, visiting the sick and shut-ins, listening to—and praying about—work and relationship troubles, and raising money, there is little time or energy left to do the things I really want to do.

Before I entered seminary a mentoring priest told me that he could do anything he wanted to do, and it could still be part of his "job." I believed him then, and I want to believe him now. But the priestly life I'd imagined, one balanced—again!—between study, writing, prayer, service, and celebration has thus far remained elusive. Much of what I do feels like burdensome duty.

At times I find myself resenting Christian men and women who don't seem to be suffering as I do as they take up the cross. At other times I think I'm a loser who is somehow missing the fun in what is surely—at bottom—a joyous occupation.

The institutional church has pitched my generation of clergy a curveball with respect to measuring success in ministry. It has become the norm in my diocese to ordain people to the priesthood who have already been through their proverbial midlife crisis. I confess to harboring some resentment that such priests are often excused from obtaining seminary educations and that they bring fat bank accounts and portable health care and retirement plans to their new jobs.

I happily concede that talented people come to priestly holy orders late in life. I thank God for their presence. But the numbers where I live are out of whack. Of eighty-nine priests in Nebraska, three are under forty. Of eight ordinations since I arrived here in 1992, one—mine—was of a person with a lifetime to commit to the priestly ministry. I do not believe that God is calling exclusively middle-aged people to the priesthood at this moment in the church (although God has done stranger things.) Rather, I believe that the Episcopal Church has an underdeveloped notion of the ministries possible for an Episcopalian experiencing spiritual renewal.

Clearly, young priests can give things to our Episcopal Church that fifty-year-old men and women cannot. Our vitality, worldview, excitement, vocational longevity, and willingness to submit to formation as priests over thirty-five or forty years are precious gifts. The sacrifice of a lifelong priesthood is a phenomenal gift and should be the norm—the measure of success—toward which we strive.

But a lifelong vocation to the priesthood is no easy job. My concern is that young priests will burn out and bail out in droves over the next four decades if we cannot support one another—in deep and meaningful ways—as we serve and are shaped by this church we love.

WASTED TALENTS

Like all Episcopalians, I am committed to—and moved by—the unique way that Christ is made known to the world in the "Anglican Way." This denomination makes Jesus real for me. Episcopalians speak my spiritual language.

And so it was with joy a few years back that I heard this comment by a zealous old senior-warden type: "The problem isn't that we have too many Episcopal priests. The problem is that we have too few Episcopal laity!" Amen, brother! Boola boola! In a similar vein, I listened enraptured to the tales of a priest friend who serves in what we delicately refer to as "greater

Nebraska." My pal happily shepherds a congregation of some twenty people who worship in a tiny church in the middle of a cornfield miles from the nearest town, all so there can be an "Anglican presence" in that corner of Nebraska's panhandle.

But Episcopal priests are set up for trouble when issued marching orders to fill only Episcopal Church pews or to promote merely the Anglican Way. My final purpose as a priest is not to create more Episcopalians but to draw more people into more meaningful relationships with Jesus Christ.

The typical Episcopal Church is a small operation. After two years serving such a "family-sized" church, I am beginning to worry about the prevailing wisdom in our denomination about "what priests are supposed to do." The small church's fight to survive is a monstrous consumer of time, treasure, and talent. In Nebraska, a priest might spend more than half the day in the car, driving between yoked mission parishes miles apart. That does not seem right. There are comparable constraints on city-dwelling, small-church clergy, such as inherited antique liturgies and crumbling "historic" plants.

There is a paradox here. I know that much of what I do probably looks to the world like "wasting time," but I know better. So do those faithful Christian people who make Bible study, prayer, meditation, deep conversation, worship, and godly play a regular part of their lives. But I am sticking to my guns in saying that, for many Episcopal priests (of all ages), the institutional church assigns duties that waste our talents.

I am not sure how to make a helpful evaluation. How many hours of driving per week is appropriate in order to be with one's people and to do the work of God? How many people need to be present at Holy Eucharist to make it "worth" saying Mass for a small community? I start with the same cherished principles of sacramental theology that have served the church well for years ("wherever two or three are gathered together in Christ's name," for example). But the presence of Christ in the midst of a tiny community does not necessarily warrant the presence of a professional, seminary-trained priest. The extreme example of a Nebraska priest at times spending half of his or her day in the car is not fiction. I do not believe that any priest should spend that much time commuting between sacramental moments.

Keeping churches open that no longer serve a significant population or need is bad stewardship. Many young priests in our Episcopal Church are becoming casualties of that mismanagement. We are called, trained, and commissioned to preach the gospel, and instead we are dispatched to run sickly small businesses. Our talent is being wasted.

It is said that one in three priests in our generation will become bishops of the church. Apparently there are so few of us that fully one-third are destined to wear a purple shirt. May God bless those of my generation who are so destined! I pray that those of us called to preside over the high councils of this church will have the courage and conviction to shut down dying churches, in full confidence of God's promise that the larger church will endure.

However, I am not interested in seeing the church follow the example of corporate America's seemingly brainless "downsizing." Rather, I hope to see discerning and intentional action on the part of our church's decision makers. I pray that tomorrow's church leaders can equip missions and parishes to share the gospel in new and exciting ways or to offer care as they are allowed to die with dignity, in the assurance that Christ will not disappear from a neighborhood because the Episcopal Church does. My concern is that my generation of priests and bishops will not have the courage to clean up the mess we've inherited and will preside over the bankruptcy and eventual death of a proud old denomination.

The Good News

If true that my first years in ministry have caused me concerns about my future in the church, I hasten to add that I have likewise been blessed, beyond measure, by the people I serve and the God I love.

Many years ago, the priest who led me to Christ said of his work, "You can't do this job unless you're ready to take a lot of strokes." In this, as in many things, the old guy was right. It is almost embarrassing to be so well loved— and so well cared for—by the very people that I am supposed to serve. I have been the recipient of wonderful gifts, both great and small, simply because I am priest to one community. I am not different from any other priest in this regard, but it is still wondrous to be on the receiving end of such care. All those acts of kindness do help convince me that what I do makes a difference. These kindnesses sustain me and make me feel good about the future.

Another astonishing blessing is being invited into people's lives at their most intimate moments. I have prayed with moms in labor and stood with dozens of couples at their weddings. I have prayed with families in the neonatal intensive care unit and attended graduation celebrations. I have baptized both young and old into Christ's family and have stood with grieving relatives at several deathbeds.

I am still amazed and, mercifully, as I get older, less embarrassed at these times. I used to worry that it was not enough to stand and witness, to pray beautiful prayers, and simply to be *present* as a symbol of Christ's loving presence. But God apparently works even through the ministry of an awkward introvert like me. And so the people keep calling for their priest. And I keep showing up. And somehow in the interchange between priest and people, Christ is made more powerful where Christ is needed most. I can only wonder how the process works and say "thank you" to the people I serve for letting me play a small part.

A final thought that gives me extraordinary hope has been a gradual introduction over the past year to the wider community of young Episcopal priests. My peers are a talented, energetic, and faithful crew. They share with me a devotion to our Anglican Way, but—perhaps in a way that is new—share a far more important and common devotion to Jesus himself. I believe that our generation of priests is committed most entirely, not to the Episcopal Church, but to Jesus Christ. I hope and pray this devotion will empower us to go the distance. While that single-minded devotion to our Lord may mean significant change for our denomination, it can only mean vitality and credibility for the church at large.

All things considered, I still feel a powerful sense of calling to ordained service in Christ's church. Although I see significant challenges ahead for myself and my young colleagues, most of the time I love this job. And even on the days when the job makes me wacky, I never doubt that I make a difference, that God approves of my efforts, and that Jesus is made more real through my sometimes clumsy efforts to be a faithful priest in our Episcopal Church.

A Living Church
Serving a Living Lord

Mission and Ministry in the Twenty-first Century

Rock H. Schuler

W e Episcopalians increasingly find ourselves swept up in a wave of enthusiasm for mission. Every day I witness a hungering for God, for the purpose and fulfillment that comes from living within and for Christ.

The divisive and traumatic issues with which our current generation of leaders must deal are not the issues of the future. On the front lines of parishes the concern is less about women priests, homosexuality, abortion, or schism—the concern has become much more fundamental. How do we as a community encounter the living presence of our risen Lord? How do we celebrate that presence in the midst of our heterogeneity—together as one people of different ages, genders, races, sexual orientations, ethnic and cultural backgrounds? How do we incorporate that presence into our daily routines? How do we act on that presence through our baptism? How do we live out our relationship with Jesus joyously and take its baptismal responsibilities seriously? In other words—How do we *live* mission?

We are coming to realize that at the core of our identity as Christians lies the mission statement of the Episcopal Church: "The mission of the Church is to restore all people to unity with God and each other in Christ" (*BCP* 855). This statement encapsulates the living union with God in Jesus that gives us true life, even as it compels us to share that fullness with those near and far—from family members and acquaintances to the whole of humanity. Love compels us to share love, and in this sharing we have life, and have it more abundantly (John 10:10b).

There are five primary ministry areas through which we do mission: (1) worship; (2) spiritual growth; (3) evangelism; (4) service; and (5) caring fellowship. These fundamental ministry areas are the true "issues" of the church's present and future. Each area will be discussed in detail, after which follows a concluding reflection on the significance of acculturation for empowerment in ministry. But first it is crucial to appreciate the importance of visionary leadership in all five areas.

VISIONARY LEADERSHIP

Just as vision is indispensable to a painter's or sculptor's art, an architect's blueprint, or a mason's brickwork, vision is the driving force behind healthy, dynamic, and productive congregational life. Vision makes the call and destiny that come from heaven sacramental, tangible, and *real*. When the rector, together with key lay leaders, beholds and articulates a clear, strong sense of direction—when they with courage own that vision and work to make it real—life-changing ministry happens. The role of parish and diocesan leadership in the twenty-first century will be to discern and pursue God's vision.

The ordained must accept responsibility for leadership. The laity have an essential ministry, both in sharing leadership and in making vision real. In the twenty-first century laypeople will play a crucial part in congregational ministry. In my parish, Holy Trinity in Lansdale, Pennsylvania, a layperson now is overseeing ministry development, and another oversees pastoral care. If parishes are to survive and prosper, this is the way of the future. But a function of the ordained is to risk, initiate, dream—to be the "point person" in discerning and articulating the vision of God for how God's mission of reconciling redemption will be pursued and realized within a particular parish and its community. The rector must lead by facilitating discernment, by bringing others into leadership roles, by putting forth ideas, by taking risks on behalf of ministry, by recognizing and calling forth the gifts of others. She must accept her responsibility as the servant-leader of the body and her role of building up that body for doing the work of God. If the rector will not lead, the parish will flounder, becoming irrelevant at best and, at worst, dead. The ordained must always exercise pastoral sensitivity. We cannot serve if we do not listen and attempt to understand.

Yet while pastoral sensitivity is needed, it must not co-opt the compassion for reaching those open to and hungry for the good news of full and eternal life in Jesus Christ. The mission of the church must not be compromised by an overly sensitive and cautious approach toward those who are out of step with or who would even undermine that mission. This is not to say that such people should be excluded, rejected, or abandoned: ministry with, among, or toward them should be attempted. But the energy spent in that pursuit must not compromise the work to which God calls us. If we remain in the towns and houses of those who have rejected us, refusing in a pastorally sensitive but ultimately futile gesture to shake the dust off our feet (Matt. 10:14), who shall share the good news among those who *are* eager and receptive? The dead must bury the dead (Matt. 8:21–22). Our call is to work among the living.

Enough said about leadership. The question is: How do we, as *leaders* of the church in the twenty-first century, guide and direct it in the fulfillment of its mission? And so we return to the previously mentioned five areas of ministry, beginning with what is primary.

WORSHIP

Worship must be at the center of our vocation as priests and as Christians. The priest's leadership position in the body derives from his sacramental position of liturgical leadership, even as the community's sacramental presence in the world derives from its encounter with Christ at the altar. The priest, beginning in and from worship, empowers the presence and work of Christ within the body so that the body can take that power and presence into the world for nothing less than its very salvation, its union with God in an eternal and transforming relationship of love.

This notion of the priest as the facilitator in worship of the community's sacramental empowerment holds the key to the shift in understanding that is occurring regarding the priest's role. The priest as liturgical and communal leader has no validity, no authenticity, apart from this renewed understanding of sacramental empowerment. The vitality of the priesthood and the future of the church herself are staked upon it. It is imperative that we understand the priest as the *one who equips the ministry of the baptized.* Such thinking has its roots in the formative theology of Ephesians, where we read that the essential nature of "apostles, prophets, evangelists, pastors, and teachers" is to "equip the saints for ministry . . ." (4:11–13).

The wellspring of this ministry lies in worship. All priests are ordained to serve the people by leading them through grace-powered worship to be all that God destines them to be. The priest's ministry of equipping the body involves, first and foremost, leading the worship of the church with an integrity and vitality that imparts a *living*—and therefore *meaningful*—experience of the risen Christ. Out of that experience with our living Lord, the people are called and empowered to fulfill their baptismal responsibilities in all five ministry areas.

Thus the people must be involved in every aspect of worship, sharing a leadership role by the invitation of rectors who neither reserve to themselves nor abdicate their liturgical responsibilities. My own parish has worked out this shared responsibility by having a liturgy team that provides invaluable input and direction. This team, composed of liturgically knowledgeable parishioners invited to be members by the rector, conducts weekly evaluations of worship services based on written congregational feedback forms provided with every service booklet. The existence of the liturgy team and the feedback opportunities help people take responsibility for the worship life of the parish. Yet to preserve the integrity of that worship life, the liturgy team, along with congregational input, is advisory only. The rector, who chairs the liturgy team, takes into account all advice and feelings, but the final decisions regarding worship and music rest with him, in keeping with Episcopal polity and canon law.[1]

An additional way to empower laity *as laity* is for lay liturgical ministers to appear in worship as laypeople, not as quasi-clerics reminiscent of minor orders. Let them be unvested! At the two new services started at my parish over the last three years, all lay ministers remain without vestment—a gesture that affirms, rather than one that implicitly denies or tries to cover up, their identity as lay servants of the presence of God. This gesture could be misunderstood if we mistakenly see the vested as the "experts" vis-à-vis God and the unvested as uninitiated amateurs. Such a misunderstanding is compounded by the usual interpretation of lay as being less than "expert." The Greek word *laos*, from which we derive *laity*, refers to "the people," which includes everyone within the body of Christ, ordained and not. Ordination does not nullify or supersede baptism, but rather "marks and shapes it" according to a particular identity and/or function within the body. The purpose of not vesting lay liturgical ministers is not to emphasize their "amateur" status, but rather to support them in their daily identity and fundamental dignity. Properly understood, vesting the ordained attests to their identity and vocation as servant-leaders set apart by and on behalf of the whole people of God; the normal garb of the laity worn in worship, properly understood, affirms them in their daily vocation as witnesses and disciples of the risen Lord. Additionally, wearing normal clothing while serving as a lay liturgical minister serves as a visible reminder that the distinction between "sacred" and "secular" is false. The laity are led by their baptism to "redeem the time" of daily life.[2]

Commissioning lay servants within the baptismal covenant also carries great symbolic weight. It publicly demonstrates that the ministry of the laity before God occurs as a part of that covenant that defines their identity and their ministry as Christian laypeople. The baptized do not need to be placed within a semi-ordained setting to be acceptable before God. They have already been accepted by God through adoption in baptism, an adoption that manifests and makes conscious God's prior and constant love for them. Several years ago we implemented such commissionings in my parish to help people understand that the context of their church-centered ministry was their baptism and not a separate rite that gave the impression of a lesser ordination. Since then, we have expanded these commissionings to include every aspect of parish life, as well as all conceivable ministries within daily life. These commissionings for daily-life ministry, celebrated four times a year according to a form developed here at Holy Trinity, have been especially valuable in helping people see their lives as nurses, technicians, researchers, parents, or gardeners as ministry in the presence and for the sake of their God. As a result, lives have been enriched and transformed. It is my prayer that practices such as we have instituted at Holy Trinity may be adopted by other parishes and dioceses.

SPIRITUAL GROWTH

Meaningful spiritual growth in the twenty-first century calls for leaders who can, like Moses, journey with the people. Priests do not stand over and above, but among. Let the ordained abandon pulpits and preach from the midst of the community, where the gospel is read and lives are lived! The difference this practice makes in conveying an immediate, personal sense of God's presence, journeying with us through life, is impossible to exaggerate. Parishioners at Holy Trinity complain vociferously whenever we have a guest preacher who uses the pulpit. As a result, our plans for a new worship space, which have developed as a response to our mission-oriented praxis and which are necessitated by parish growth, do not include a pulpit (or, for that matter, an organ!).

And let the clergy's sermons address real-life concerns and practical spirituality. Doing so means that we are willing to live with ambiguity. Such is the age in which we live—ambiguous. The twenty-first-century priest must be comfortable with ambiguity and help the community grow spiritually and do mission effectively in the midst of the church's own moral and existential uncertainties. We do not need to hold tenaciously to ideological, political, or theological positions in order to do mission together. Such jaundiced attitudes often reflect interior insecurity. Better that twenty-first-century priests maintain positions in the belief that they are right while accepting that they could be wrong. Better that twenty-first-century priests remain open to an ever greater measure of truth that more closely approximates actual Truth. Such attitudes make us more humble, better able to live and work with and to learn from those with whom we may disagree.

Spiritual growth entails "daily-life ministry"—an understanding that our baptism necessitates living our Christian vocation in every arena of life. Each program area of our parish, from Christian education to baptismal formation to pastoral care, is designed to equip, empower, and enable people to live as Christians in every moment of their lives.

The foundation of this empowerment is our lay ministry development program. Lay ministry at Holy Trinity flows out of the catechumenate, which prepares people in a deliberate and extensive way for their own baptism or for the baptism of their children. Baptisms are then celebrated with style— with superb and joyous music, dynamic sermons, and the full and rich use of symbolism. We employ oversized, illuminated certificates signed in multiple colors by all worshipers; engraved, enlarged, personal baptismal candles; a liberal use of water, in which infants are immersed, or which is poured over adults (our new worship space will have full immersion); chrism generously bestowed upon the heads of the newly baptized; receptions at which cake, punch, and laughter freely flow. We have found that such conscientious Christian formation and initiation enriches and deepens the whole parish's relationship with Jesus.

Based on the model of the catechumenate are our SEARCH groups— small, catechetical support groups designed to nurture and renew the baptismal spirituality of Christians. These groups are focused on the same objectives as the catechumenate—deepening prayer, understanding scripture, appreciating community, learning to do justice and peace within the framework of human dignity. If justice and peace are to be accomplished in a way that enhances human dignity, then it must be understood that lay ministry goes far beyond the immediate church community. We emphasize that the heart of the ministry of the laity lies not within Sunday worship but within the weekly world. We conduct a short, four-session seminar that helps people appreciate this connection between their Christian faith and their daily life at home or at work. The seminar is based on Bill Diehl's book *The Monday Connection*.[3] Beyond the seminar, we offer a long-term support group for the living of Christian faith within the world, which we call Practicing the Monday Connection. These groups, deliberately meeting outside of the church building, review case studies and offer prayer to be empowered to act as Christians in worldly situations. Such study intends that time itself be redeemed, that none of it be compartmentalized and thus separated from God's reconciling love, that we as Christians do truly live, as the Orthodox theologian Alexander Schmemann put it, "for the life of the world."

Christianity cannot be taken for granted. It is time to call and equip the people to live out their baptismal relationship with Jesus socially, vocationally, politically, economically, relationally. Either we believe the baptismal covenant and take it seriously, or we don't. Lukewarm is not an option (Rev. 3:16).

EVANGELISM

This equipping, "building-up" theology carries into evangelism, outreach, and fellowship. In each area the responsibility and joy of the priest is to empower and enable people to do ministry, to move a congregation from a maintenance mind-set to a mission orientation.

Two critical observations regarding the empowerment of the laity to do evangelism: (1) the people must appreciate that they are, by virtue of baptism, *evangelists*; and (2) they must have a healthy understanding of that role.

To these ends, my parish has made evangelism the focus of our ministry efforts. The empowerment of the laity in every aspect of our parish program is designed to fulfill the church's mission of universal reconciliation with God, which will then result in universal reconciliation within creation. Everything we do is structured to "make known by word and deed the love of the crucified and risen Christ in the power of the Holy Spirit, so that people will repent, believe, and receive Christ as their Savior and obediently serve him as their Lord in the fellowship of his Church" (Anglican Primates' Definition of Evangelism).

As a result, we preach the necessity of witnessing to Christ, of inviting those without a relationship with Jesus to come into and experience his love. We offer an evangelism training seminar, "New Life through Evangelism." This training gives people a theological grounding, helping them to see evangelism not as judgmental but as incarnational. This particularly Anglican approach to mission sees its purpose as bringing to light and to fulfillment the preexisting presence of God within the life of another. As Jesus said, "The kingdom of God is within you!" (Luke 17:21).

We also have an extensive church-growth team, with a significant budget (almost 5 percent of parish income), that reminds the parish how to be welcoming, that makes sure guests are greeted, contacted after worship, and incorporated. This team receives top billing at our vestry meetings, reporting before all other business, as a way of highlighting its crucial role. The team looks continually at every aspect of the parish's life not only for ways to "market" our ministries and to plan for growth but for ways by which we can ensure that every parish program is connected to the community.

SERVICE

Empowering the people to do outreach is to empower them to do evangelism through specific deeds. A few years back the large rooming house that stands next to our church went up for sale. A parishioner talked with me about the possibility of purchasing the home as a transitional housing center for needy individuals. After looking into the possibility, the outreach team and I determined that it would make an ideal transitional center for homeless men. I then preached a sermon dedicated to the idea, announcing that Holy Trinity would commit $25,000 of its current capital campaign to the project. At the time, we did not have the money in hand, nor did we have parish or vestry support. The sermon was designed to stimulate excitement and generate that support.

Our every effort was then thrown into the project and raising funds. More than a year later, we had purchased the $200,000 home in conjunction with a local housing authority. Soon thereafter, we began renovations and saw our first tenants arrive. When all was said and done, Holy Trinity had contributed more than $25,000, but of that amount only $8,000 came from capital funds. The balance came from unsolicited donations by parishioners. Ezra House, as we came to call it, proved to be a textbook case in empowering the laity to do outreach. Currently we are exploring ways to reach out in Christian witness and welcome to the residents of Ezra—integrating outreach and evangelism.

Leadership that empowers is about discerning where God is active, getting on board with that activity, and then leading others into it. It is about vision, and the hard work of commitment.

CARING FELLOWSHIP

Such vision and commitment is essential in fellowship, as in the other ministry areas. Unfortunately, many parishioners seem to regard fellowship as the least flashy of the five. It involves a minimal amount of bells and whistles and requires perhaps the most drudge work—setting up tables, wiping off tablecloths, putting out food, cleaning out the refrigerator, washing dishes, and so on. Yet experience has taught me that, without fellowship, all other ministry efforts fall flat. If people do not find the love and support of Christian community in worship, they will stop attending. If they do not find that love and support among the Christians with whom they associate, they will cease to look to the church for spiritual growth. If fellowship is absent from evangelism and outreach programs, the programs do nothing to reconcile people by creating relationships. Instead the programs become little more than ecclesiastical bureaucracies. We have spent an enormous amount of effort and expense on fellowship at Holy Trinity. An intrinsic aspect of our evangelism programs, like the alternative, Thursday evening "Rite III" worship, or our monthly orientation dinners, is the sharing of food—often a prerequisite to effective fellowship. Our baptisms are always followed by a social gathering.

For a modest, at-cost fee we provide a continental breakfast on Sundays and a weekly parish dinner on Saturdays (after the 5 P.M. Eucharist). Food flows freely at almost every Holy Trinity event, and child care is always available. Opportunities are continually presented for people to get to know each other, or to become better acquainted—foyer groups, parish trips, special church school events, and so on.

Having elaborated on each of the five ministry areas essential to Holy Trinity's life and mission, I conclude with thoughts on the increasingly compelling task of acculturation in effective, successful mission.

MINISTRY EMPOWERMENT AND ACCULTURATION

It is crucial to grasp the change this ministry-empowering orientation will bring to the life of the church. A mission-centered, ministry-enabling church must be able to relate to the culture in which it is located. Like Paul, the church must be all things to all people in order to transmit effectively the healing life of Jesus Christ. On the surface, therefore, the church will look much like its culture. Only by relating to and infiltrating the culture can we hope to effect change within the lives of the people and institutions of society. Acculturation is a critical topic for the whole Anglican Communion. Without it, we are irrelevant. This means that it is time fully to Americanize our church. But we must be careful: if the purpose of mission is not kept clear, we will be absorbed.

An Americanized Episcopal church will, like our society, be diverse. Parishes will reflect the neighborhoods in which they are located, the multiple and rich cultures in which they find themselves. Intentional efforts to foster and reflect such diversity will be undertaken. Liturgical and musical styles will be altered, as will vestments and color schemes, even prayers and architecture.

At Holy Trinity, we have been and are facing questions surrounding acculturation. A few years ago, when our electronic organ gave out (thanks be to God!), we used the opportunity to reformat our music to a contemporary Christian vein, complete with band, modern instruments, and a new sound system. Additionally, we have updated and made more relevant the Prayers of the People, and we have drawn freely on the supplemental Eucharistic prayers. From our stained glass windows, to the hymns we select, to the vestments we wear, to the signs in front of our building, to the doors of our church, we have struggled with how best to reflect, and thus to infiltrate and transform, our cultural environment.

Often working against us, and against the whole of our church, is English cultural propriety and elitism. These traits are revealed in our church by what I have heard called the 2 percent rule, which maintains that, because the Episcopal Church includes about 2 percent of the overall population, we cannot appeal to more than 2 percent of the population in any given area. If we assume a highly complex and literate liturgy with a strong dose of Edwardian stuffiness, the 2 percent rule may be generous! Without acculturation, the Anglican Communion dooms itself to become a church of Anglophiles and English expatriates, most of whom never come to worship.

But with acculturation, the 2 percent rule is shattered. We must not repeat the mistakes of the past and exclude ourselves from carrying the good news of Christ in whatever form and with whatever tools prove effective. I am not suggesting that we abandon our unique identity in the name of popularity. I am saying that we must look for opportunities to translate what we have been given as Episcopalians in ways that people of our time can understand, appreciate, and accept. We must not fear betraying our English cultural roots—only the person and message of Jesus Christ!

In keeping with the medley that is our society, the Episcopal Church should create worship services designed for the culture or cultures of a neighborhood or area—even to the point, as at Holy Trinity, of having a large variety of worship services within one parish. Holy Trinity has established four unique worship events, all using different prayers and music. To reach as broad a population as possible, each service has a different "feel" that appeals to different sorts of folks. There is a traditional early Rite I service, with two or three traditional hymns accompanied by organ music; a later Rite II service with both contemporary and traditional music, in which traditional hymns are set to modern instruments; a Saturday evening contemporary service that uses supplemental texts; and a Thursday evening alternative "Rite III" service held in the parish hall with a rock band. We continue to seek new ways to revise and improve our services. In the year 2000, for instance, we plan to implement a multimedia 11:15 A.M. service geared to young singles and couples, using a mix of our Thursday and Saturday services.

If it is to thrive and not merely survive, the Episcopal Church in the twenty-first century will use worship resources designed around a common structure and a minimum set of requirements that the larger church considers essential to eucharistic celebrations. "Rite III"–type worship, set within a palette of contemporary musical formats, will become normative in churches and dioceses. The days of a standard *Book of Common Prayer* and hymnal with a universal liturgy are beginning to end. The days of multiple worship opportunities to serve the needs of particular people, while staying centered on our unity within the person and presence of Jesus Christ, are starting to begin.

As Episcopalians we are uniquely situated to address the growing tension in our society between personal and group rights and responsibilities. A church that reflects and speaks to our culture must live creatively within this tension. As a communal religion with a high regard for the dignity of every person, there is much that is helpful in the Episcopal tradition.

At Holy Trinity, we have attempted to honor both common responsibility and individual rights by creating a parish "Rule of Life," which all leaders must sign and try to live by. This Rule has even been incorporated into our parish bylaws as the official standard of parish membership, although we make clear that people are expected to be journeying toward the goal rather than to have arrived. We also make it clear to new parishioners that they are welcome to walk with us for as long as they like before deciding to reaffirm their baptism publicly and to take the Rule seriously as their personal standard. The idea behind the Rule is to achieve a broad sense of responsibility for our parish vision by joining in a common spiritual discipline—centered on the baptismal covenant—that includes the parish vision statement, prayer, Bible reading, spiritual reflection and guidance, and financial tithing. But within this broad framework is much latitude for personalizing the Rule. Our expectation is that we are all working toward the same end but not necessarily in the same way.

An Americanized Episcopal Church will also have increasingly informal worship services, demonstrating an ease and comfort not known in many of our parishes. Worship will be "user-friendly"—especially for children and guests. But worship will be professional, delivered with precision and care. Much can be learned from the media. It is possible to make people feel at ease while conducting a top-rate "production" that draws them in as active participants. Attentiveness to the liturgy is required, including willingness to spend time in preparation as well as money on musicians and quality "props." Chief among these requirements will be a service book that each week contains the entire liturgy. At Holy Trinity, we have found that this task gets numerous people involved in parish life and enhances fellowship. Use of the service book makes the liturgy far more accessible to both members and guests. We should also be willing as a church to use professional multimedia capabilities, incorporating pictures, video, and computer graphics into our services even as we use the Internet and other modern technology to convey our vision of Christ.

Of course, worship is far more than a production. The theatrical terms above are used in a metaphorical sense only. Worship is indeed an "iconic" experience that is a foretaste of heavenly life. It is the font from which the Holy Spirit sustains the world. Even as we incorporate the contemporary in an effort to reach society in a meaningful way, we must bear in mind the eternal perspective of the church—a perspective held in trust within our worship services—and avoid an acculturation that leaves no transforming substance in its wake. The idea is to infiltrate and transform the lives of people, and the life of our society—not to be absorbed ourselves.

Yet this is all the more reason to exceed the culture in our professionalism while crafting a warm and inviting worship atmosphere that welcomes. An icon is of little value if there are none to pray before it. We must be willing to engage the congregation, to talk with them, to converse in the sermon, to clap and laugh and have fun, to let the kids dance in the aisles and sing to the music—all within the context of a well-planned, meticulously produced worship experience. In this way we will plant the seeds that bear the fruit of reconciliation with God. As American Episcopalians, we will be adventurous, purposeful risk-takers, believing that the journey through the wilderness or the return from exile are motifs befitting much of our culture.

One final question: What, in the future, will make us Episcopalians? If not our English cultural identity or the *Book of Common Prayer* or the universality of our worship, then what? In the future our primary concern will be to be Christian. The ecumenical movement must be given top priority as we enter into a world decidedly apathetic, if not hostile, to Christianity. We must compromise and accommodate as necessary in order to stand united as we seek to accomplish the mission of Christ. Like it or not, the church is becoming a Christian subculture, with less of a direct influence upon the broader society. We need to adapt to this reality and strengthen our common identity.

Nevertheless, there is much that we will hold onto and contribute as Episcopalians: our incarnational, sacramental approach to spirituality, leading to a strong concern for the here-and-now and a deep appreciation of God's transcendence made present through beauty and within creation; acculturation, an Anglican principle since the Celtic church, evident in Pope Gregory's instructions to Augustine of Canterbury regarding the treatment of pagan religious sites and practices, or Cranmer's setting of the liturgy in English, or the *American Prayer Book* after the Revolution; and the *via media*, our ability to see in broad accommodation and inclusivity the essence of truth, which is always larger than, and somewhat different from, what we imagined. Yet the *via media* has never been "anything goes." It is set within boundaries: an intolerance of attacks against human dignity, for example, or an unwillingness to depart from the Nicene Creed. Adhering to Jesus Christ within the historic faith of Christianity while offering our unique understandings about sacramentality, acculturation, and the *via media* will be the core of Anglican identity in the twenty-first century.

By doing ministry in the five highlighted areas within the context of our culture, we can advance the mission of the church, satisfying the hunger of the people with the living vitality of Jesus Christ!

NOTES

1. See *Constitution and Canons*, Canons II.5 and III.14
2. This logic holds true as an argument for unvesting the ordained as well, who function within worship to incarnate the presence of Christ within the body. An incarnational act like presiding without vestments could, in some contexts, bolster the message that all of the baptized are to "redeem the time" together. This is the rationale my parish uses for not having the clergy vest at one of the four main services. At the others we feel the beauty of the liturgy as a reflection of the glory of God, and the identity of the priestly servant-leader as described above is well-served by the vestments.
3. Bill Diehl, *The Monday Connection: On Being an Authentic Christian in a Weekday World* (San Francisco: HarperSanFrancisco, 1993).

AFTERWORD

Continuing the Conversation, Continuing the Conversion

N. J. A. Humphrey

The nature of this book renders it timebound. The contributors address specific issues that we believe important to the future of the church, but we also recognize that these issues will change as the years pass. Other issues will replace them, just as the debates over the divinity of Christ gave way to the iconoclastic controversy, which in turn gave way to Reformation-era debates about papal authority. In relatively recent history, the issue of slavery has given way to the civil rights movement, the ordination of women, and that hottest of hot topics: sexuality. All of these will pass away. Indeed, heaven and earth will pass away (Rev. 21:1).

But relationships founded in Christ Jesus will not pass away. They grow and mature as the Spirit infuses the body with new life. So while today I may converse with my sister in Christ about inclusive language in the liturgy and doctrinal orthodoxy, twenty years from now who knows what we'll be talking about? The point is to keep talking—and more important, to keep listening.

So now that we've had our say, it's our turn to listen. To provide a forum for readers and essayists to continue the conversation, we encourage you to visit the Web site of Gathering the NeXt Generation at http://www.gtng.org. We may also be available for speaking engagements, visits to parishes, diocesan centers, seminaries, retreats, and conferences. If interested in making such arrangements, E-mail us at GTNGBook@gtng.org, or separately through the E-mail addresses listed in the "Notes on Contributors." Through this book we want to gather the next generation, not just dust on a library shelf.

NOTES ON CONTRIBUTORS

J. Scott Barker (b. 1963) is Vicar of the Episcopal Church of the Resurrection in Omaha, Nebraska. He received his B.A. in Religious Studies from Yale College in 1985, his M.Div. from Yale Divinity School, and his Diploma in Anglican Studies from Berkeley Divinity School at Yale in 1992. He was ordained in the Diocese of Omaha in 1992. Scott is married to his college sweetheart, Annie, and has two children, ages 6 and 8. Barker@gtng.org

Jennifer Lynn Baskerville (b. 1966) currently serves as Associate for Christian Formation at St. Peter's Episcopal Church in Morristown, New Jersey. She was sponsored for ordination by the Episcopal Church at Cornell and was ordained to the priesthood at thirty-one in the Diocese of Central New York. Jennifer earned her A.B. from Smith College, an M.A. in historic preservation from Cornell University, and an M.Div. from the Church Divinity School of the Pacific. In her spare time she serves as a preservation consultant and enjoys tennis, rowing, and mountain biking. Baskerville@gtng.org

Daniel Emerson Hall (b. 1969) is currently a resident in General Surgery at the University of Pittsburgh Medical Center. Sponsored by the Diocese of Connecticut, he was ordained a transitional deacon in June 1999 and is currently associated with Trinity Cathedral in Pittsburgh. Daniel studied at Yale University, earning degrees from the College, Divinity School, and Medical School, as well as a Diploma in Anglican Studies from Berkeley Divinity School at Yale. Before entering graduate school, he taught biology and chemistry at a mission school in Zimbabwe. When not in the operating room or the pulpit, he enjoys ultimate Frisbee, fishing, and singing. Hall@gtng.org

Nathan Humphrey (b. 1973) received his B.A. from St. John's College in Annapolis, Maryland, known for its unique "Great Books" curriculum (www.sjca.edu). He received an M.Div. (*magna cum laude*) from Yale Divinity School and a Diploma in Anglican Studies from Berkeley Divinity School at Yale. One of the joys of this project was editing the book during Clinical Pastoral Education (CPE) at Johns Hopkins Hospital in Baltimore. He is currently Chaplain to the Washington Episcopal School in the Diocese of

Washington (D.C.) and an aspirant for Holy Orders in the Diocese of Maryland. He lives in Bethesda, Maryland, with his cat, Monica, named after St. Augustine's mother. When not editing essays he enjoys swing, waltz, NPR, *The Simpsons*, and MTV. Humphrey@gtng.org

Richard Kew (b. 1945) is qualified to contribute to this volume because he believes passionately in tomorrow's generation providing leadership and has parented two GenXers! Born, raised, trained, and ordained in England, he moved from the Church of England to the Episcopal Church in 1976. He has served in three U.S. dioceses, and in parishes and paraparochial organizations. As founding chair of the South American Missionary Society and director of other mission ventures, his interests and involvements are global. His previous publications include *No Foothold in the Swamp: A Story of One Man's Burnout in Ministry* (Zondervan, 1988); *Starting Over, but Not from Scratch: Mental and Spiritual Health Between Jobs* (Abingdon, 1995); with Cyril Okorocha, *Vision Bearers: Dynamic Evangelism in the Twenty-first Century* (Morehouse, 1996); and with Roger White, *New Millennium, New Church: Trends Shaping the Episcopal Church for the Twenty-first Century* (Cowley, 1992); *Venturing into the New Millennium* (Latimer, 1994); and *Toward 2015: A Church Odyssey* (Cowley, 1997). At present the Director of the Anglican Forum for the Future, he resides with his wife, Rosemary, a college professor, in Murfreesboro, Tennessee. Kew@gtng.org

Jamie E. L'Enfant (b. 1967) is Assistant Rector at Holy Trinity Episcopal Church in Greensboro, North Carolina. She received a B.A. in philosophy from Louisiana State University, an M.Div. from the Divinity School at Duke University, and an S.T.M. in Anglicanism from the General Theological Seminary in New York. Sponsored by the Diocese of North Carolina, she was ordained deacon in 1995 and priest in 1996. She lives with her husband, Chris Rachal, and their cats. LEnfant@gtng.org

Christopher Martin (b. 1968), the founder and coleader of Gathering the NeXt Generation, is the Assistant Rector for Young Adult Ministries at All Saints' Church, Beverly Hills, California. He previously served as Curate at Christ Church Cathedral, Hartford, Connecticut, as a consultant to the Evangelism Office of the Episcopal Church Center, and, before seminary, as Children's and Youth Ministry Director at St. Mark's Cathedral, Seattle. He received his B.A. in philosophy and theatre studies and M.Div. (*cum laude*) from Yale University, and a Diploma in Anglican Studies from Berkeley Divinity School at Yale. Sponsored by the Diocese of Olympia, he was ordained deacon in 1996 and priest in 1997. Married since 1992 to Chloe Drake, he enjoys poetry, eating, drinking wine, and playing ultimate Frisbee. Martin@gtng.org

Beth Maynard (b. 1962) grew up unchurched in Nashville, Tennessee. After a conversion to Christ through the Episcopal Church in her late teens, she graduated from Amherst College and worked first in music publishing and then as director of a shelter for the homeless. Ordained from the Diocese of Massachusetts in 1994, after receiving an M.Div. (*summa cum laude*) from Boston University School of Theology and doing an "Anglican year" at Seabury-Western Theological Seminary, she has served parishes in the Dioceses of West Virginia and Massachusetts. She is the author of *Meditations for Lay Eucharistic Ministers*, part of Morehouse's Faithful Servant series. Maynard@gtng.org

Kate Moorehead (b. 1970) is the Rector of St. Margaret's Church in Boiling Springs, South Carolina. She received a B.A. from Vassar College and an M.Div. from Virginia Theological Seminary. Sponsored by the Diocese of Connecticut, she was ordained deacon in 1997 and priest in 1998. Kate loves to put her son Luke in a backpack and go hiking with her husband, J. D., and their two Labrador retrievers. Moorehead@gtng.org

Rock H. Schuler (b. 1965) received a B.S. in Political Economics from the University of Wyoming and an M.Div. and D.Min. from Seabury-Western Theological Seminary. Ordained deacon in 1990 and priest in 1991 in the Diocese of Wyoming, he has served as Vicar of St. Andrew's, Meeteetse, Wyoming; as Assistant Rector of St. Mark's, Casper, Wyoming; and is presently Rector of Holy Trinity, Lansdale, Pennsylvania. He is married to Patricia LaFountain; they have twin daughters, Leia and Rebecca, 12. Schuler@gtng.org

Margaret K. Schwarzer (b. 1963) is the Episcopal Chaplain at Boston University in the Diocese of Massachusetts. She received her B.A. with honors in English from Smith College, an M.Div. from Yale Divinity School, and a Diploma in Anglican Studies from Berkeley Divinity School at Yale. Sponsored by the Diocese of Washington, she was ordained to the priesthood in 1994 at Trinity Church in Princeton, New Jersey, where she served as Assistant Minister for three years. Schwarzer@gtng.org

Benjamin Shambaugh (b. 1963) is the rector of St. John's Episcopal Church in the Diocese of Washington. He received a B.A. with honors from Northwestern University, and an M.Div. from the General Theological Seminary in New York. Sponsored by the Diocese of Chicago, he was ordained deacon and priest in 1988. His career has included ministry in the national parks, the West Indies, and most recently Europe, where he served as Canon Pastor of the American Cathedral in Paris. Married to Shari Goddard, he is the father of two children, and in his spare time enjoys tuba playing and home-improvement projects. Shambaugh@gtng.org

Nancy Alane Gorman Vogele (b. 1963) is the Associate Rector of St. Matthew's Church in Goffstown, New Hampshire. She received a B.A. from Dartmouth College in 1985, an M.Div. from Yale Divinity School in 1994, a Diploma in Anglican Studies from Berkeley Divinity School at Yale in 1993, and a D.Min. (with a focus on re-visioning mission) from Episcopal Divinity School in 1999. Sponsored by the Diocese of New Hampshire, she was ordained deacon in 1993 and priest in 1994. She is also a member of the Concord Area (N.H.) Task Force against Racism and Intolerance, an adult facilitator for Concord Outright (a group for gay, lesbian, bisexual, transgendered, and questioning youth), and is the U.S. Commissary for the Anglican Church of the Congo. She plays the fiddle and is currently learning African drumming. Vogele@gtng.org

Acknowledgments

J. Scott Barker: *I would like to thank Annie, Em, and Sam for supporting me in a vocation about which they have had little choice. I would also like to thank Rev. Greg Rickel for helping me clarify my ideas about "wasted talents" and the ministries of second-career priests.*

Jennifer Lynn Baskerville: *I thank Rev. Gayle Harris and Rev. Reginald Payne-Wiens for allowing their ordination stories to form the heart of the essay. Rev. Theodora Brooks and Rev. C. John Thompson-Quartey also deserve thanks for their willingness to be interviewed. My essay is dedicated to all those, clergy and lay, Black and white, who have raised up and supported young Black men and women for ordination.*

Daniel Emerson Hall: *I wish to make special mention of Christopher Martin, Elizabeth Hall, Ashley Beasley, and Nathan Humphrey.*

Nathan Humphrey: *As editor, I have quite a few people to acknowledge, both for my own essay and for the project as a whole. First among them are the essayists themselves, of course. Two essayists who are also "GenX/COMers" provided valuable assistance in editing my essay: Jamie L'Enfant and Nancy Vogele. For their contributions to the project as a whole, I want to acknowledge Christopher Martin, Beth Maynard, Richard Kew, and Dan Hall. I would like to thank Rt. Rev. John Rabb and those members of the Commission on Ministry in my diocese who read and commented on my essay: Rev. Deacon Lauren Welch, Rev. Chris Tang (another GenX/COMer), and Rev. Nick MacDonald. Thanks also go out to the people and priests of St. Anne's, Annapolis, Maryland, particularly Rev. John Price, Rev. Ann Burts, and the members of my lay committee: Shannon and Maggie McDowell, Marilyn Roper, Ned Criscimagna, and Maura Tennor. At Epiphany, Odenton, Maryland, I would like to thank Rev. Phebe McPherson and Toni Graff, both of whom unwittingly provided grist for the mill. At St. Paul's, Huntington, Connecticut, I want to thank Rev. Tom Furrer and parishioners for their moral and financial support. Rev. Dr. Rowan Greer, Dr. Robert Martin, and Fr. Richard Chiola provided valuable insights essential to this entire collection* *while I was their student at Yale Divinity School. I thank also the brothers of the Society of St. John the Evangelist, in whose Cambridge, Massachusetts, guesthouse I conceived the idea for this collection, and the monks of Mount Saviour Monastery in Elmira, New York, in whose guesthouse I gave birth to my own essay. The influence of Suzanne Farnham will be evident to all who read my essay, as will that of the Listening Hearts Discernment Group she assembled on my behalf: Jeannine Ruof, Lee Owen, and John Seeley. This list would be incomplete without special thanks to my spiritual father, Rt. Rev. David Leighton, and his wife, Carolyn. For support and ample inspiration I thank CPE of Baltimore, Inc., at Johns Hopkins Hospital. I thank my supervisors, Rev. Marla Coulter-McDonald and Rev. P. Barrett Rudd, and my fellow CPE chaplain interns: Rev. Deacon Eric Zile, Rev. Tricia McClendon, Sue Koenig, Bryce Formwalt, and Clyde Spicer. Drs. Sheila M. Barry, Stewart Bramson, and David Cowie deserve special mention. And, of course, this project would not have happened without the support of my family: my parents, Rev. David Gleason Humphrey and Lois Humphrey, and siblings Paul and Anna, who've often seen the logs in my eye. I thank also my E-mailing grandparents and Marilyn Humphrey. Finally, I wish to thank the community of St. John's College in Annapolis Maryland, particularly the staff and student aides of the library and the admissions office; I wish to make special mention of Lisa Richmond, Robin Falcone, John Christensen, Dorcey Rose, Dave Cherry, Mary Colby, Cathy Hughes, and Hermes Bojhaxhi, the latter two of whom provided essential technical support. Any incompleteness in this list should be attributed to its ostentatious length and the limits set thereon.*

Jamie E. L'Enfant: *For their encouragement, I thank my husband, Chris Rachal, and my father, Howard L'Enfant. For her early influence and lasting impression, my continued gratitude goes to Rev. Alice Babin. For being a mentor, friend, and comrade in arms, I am most grateful to Rev. John L. Jenkins. And for being my bishop, I wish to thank Rt. Rev. Robert C. Johnson, Jr.*

Christopher Martin: *I want to thank Christine McSpadden, Mike Kinman, and Bill Danaher for being such great "teammates." Also topping the list are my wife, Chloe Martin, and Very Rev. Dick Mansfield and the people of Christ Church Cathedral, Hartford, for their support. And, of course, I want to thank Nathan Humphrey for the initiative and the hard and persistent work of pulling this project together.*

Beth Maynard: *Those who read and commented on early drafts of this essay were Robert Woodroofe III, Jessica Clark, and Mark Dirksen.*

Kate Moorehead: *I thank especially J. D. Moorehead; St. John's Church in West Hartford; Cynthia Goetz, our nurse-midwife; Rt. Rev. Clarence Coleridge; Very Rev. Martha Horne; Rev. Susan Sharpe; and Rev. Kathy Lewis.*

Margaret Schwarzer: *My essay is dedicated to Rev. Philip Zaeder and Rev. Ms. Lee McGee, mentors and friends, who believed in my authority when I was very young. I am also grateful to Right Rev. Thomas Shaw, S.S.J.E., and the Diocese of Massachusetts for their passionate commitment to the spiritual life of young adults.*

Ben Shambaugh: *I thank Shari, my wife; the staff, vestry, and people of St. John's Church, Olney; as well as Rev. Ruth Ferguson, Assistant Rector, St. John's, Olney; Very Rev. Ernest Hunt, Dean of the American Cathedral in Paris; and Rev. Canon Henry "Jack" Childs, Interim Dean of the American Cathedral. I also thank Rt. Rev. Jeffery Rowthorn, Rt. Rev. John Krumm, and Rt. Rev. Matthew Bigliardi, Bishops of the Convocation of American Episcopal Churches in Europe during my tenure there, and finally, Rt. Rev. J. Clark Grew, Bishop of Ohio and rector during my curacy.*

Visit us at www.gtng.org or E-mail us at the addresses listed in the "Notes on Contributors" section.